Name Colorology
Key to Your
Beauty, Personality, Romance & Success!

By

Baron Paul Greycastle

By Baron Greycastle

Baron Paul Greycastle has been involved in the color and fashion fields for over 25 years. He has analyzed colors and designed garments for department stores, exclusive boutiques, corporations, and individuals in the entertainment field. He has lectured at numerous educational and medical institutions, and is also listed as president of "National Color Day" in the Chase national events calendar. Mr. Greycastle is being referred to as the "Color King", "Super Stylist", and the next "Super Guru", by experts in many fields. Presently he is continuing his studies on the effects of colors in relation to human character traits and creating a, "Whole New Industry", based on his Name Colorology philosophy. He has proven, and you will see by the facts and figures in this book, that people's names and the colors that are attuned to their names affect every aspect of their lives; spiritual, mental, vocal, physical, control, emotional and sexual. Experts are saying that Mr. Greycastle has discovered the "greatest beauty philosophy of all time."

Mr.Greycastle is also a strong supporter of a ban on using fur, leather, and any other fabrics in fashion or home furnishing that cause harm and unnecessary pain to animals. A percentage of all sales of his books and other Name Colorology products will be donated to animal rights endeavors. He says we should all use God's example of saving the different species when he had Noah gather up all the species of animals when he flooded the earth. They are here for good reasons.

For further information regarding individual, home, or business consultations for full color services you can contact us at:

Name Colorology Group
P O Box 21
Crockett, CA. 94525

www.namecolorology.com
Toll Free 1-877-505 9100

NAME COLOROLOGY
Key to Your Beauty, Personality, Romance & Success

Author: Baron Paul Greycastle
Publisher: Name Colorology Group, P.O. Box 21, Crockett, CA 94525
ISBN Number 0-9621693-8-2
Library of Congress Control Number - 2001098627

All names used in this book are intended for reference only.

(THE INFORMATION IN THIS BOOK IS FOR ENTERTAINMENT PURPOSES. BEFORE USING ANY OF THE FORMULA'S OR EXERCISES IN THIS BOOK CONSULT WITH YOUR PHYSICIAN. USING ANY INFORMATION IN THIS BOOK WILL BE AT YOUR OWN RISK.)

Printed in China
Cover design and color concept by Baron Paul Greycastle
Cover design graphics by Kien Tran
e-mail kbt157@pacbell.net
Photography by Jamie Hardin and Barry Evans Studio, Pinole CA
Makeup by Valerie Smith
Garments made by Olga Harley, Patti Amerine and Jackie Slack
Book Layout by Unique Printing, Richmond, CA

Names alone mock destruction; they survive the doom of all creation. -Trevanion.

PREFACE

I would like to clarify from the start that my Name Colorology theory is in no way intended to replace any form of Biblical teaching. My theory is that God creates all things and they are gifts given to us to use on a daily basis to enrich our lives and also to help us through our good and troubled times. I believe God made colors and gave us our seven spiritual centers for very specific reasons to be used for our benefit, which I will explain through my research and theory in this book.

In Biblical quotes we are told, "Know thyself", and, "You are the light of the world". I believe through my discoveries that your name and colors determines 70% or more of your personality and talents of your seven energy personality centers; spiritual, mental, vocal, physical, control, emotional, and sexual. By learning this philosophy you are fulfilling this command "to know thyself". It is a known fact that "light" broken down contains the seven spectrums of colors, therefore this leads us to investigate further the spiritual character traits of colors and light. It is also in Biblical teachings that man was made in God's image, what is God's image? It is his positive and wonderful character attributes, such as compassion, fairness, faith, forgiveness, giving, honesty, intellect, joy, kindness, love, loyalty, peace, understanding, warmth and many other character attributes that are attuned to the colors of the spectrum that are listed in this book. God wants us to cultivate these positive traits to create the same images that he lives by. He knows that if we cultivate these traits we will live happier and wholesome lives and the world will be a happier and more peaceful place for us to live. You will find out in this book how your name is attuned to God's character attributes and how you can cultivate them.

"A man's name is not like a mantle which merely hangs about him, and which one perchance may safely twitch and pull, but a perfect fitting garment, which, like skin, has grown over him, at which one cannot rake and scrape without injuring the man himself." -Goethe.

I would like to point out that God's spirit should be in every aspect of our lives including all industries such as advertising, art, beauty, career consulting, education, entertainment, fashion, finance, home decorating, literature, marriage consultants, medical, science, sports, etc.

Most of us will agree that in this age our society has become degenerated in many ways. From the lack of God's spirit in our society, we can see a result of spiritual darkness such as drugs, stress, unfairness, violence, etc. It is common knowledge that people are suffering from depression, drug addiction, health and financial problems on a large and accelerated pace.

The purpose of exposing the light is to help individuals to come into harmony with, "God's Rainbow" of spiritual character attributes and the seven energy centers that God has given us. These will help them to recognize a moral and balanced way of living in their daily lives. The moral fiber of God will help to free one of wrongful addictions, therefore uplifting ones spirit and overcoming the trappings of spiritual darkness and sinful nature.

Man's knowledge of color is limited. Through my research and others before me, presently the light of God can be broken down into seven spectrums of color. Within these seven spectrums each tint, true hue, and shade of colors can be broken down further to reflect many of God's character attributes that he has given to us. I have found that through the vibration sounds of the different letters in our names are connected to the seven colors of the spectrum. This then determines our character attributes, talents, and the harmony of these colors to our seven energy centers, which I will elaborate on, in detail, further in this book.

Some of the basic formulas in this second book are the same as my first book, but there are many new discoveries, greatly improved photographs, garments, a greater variety of color fan colors, and most importantly there is a greater acknowledgment of God's spiritual color attributes.

"Science can only be created by those thoroughly imbued with the aspiration toward truth and understanding. This source of feeling, however, springs from the sphere of religion, science without religion is lame, religion without science is blind." -Albert Einstein

CONTENTS

INTRODUCTION

After many years of interest in the aspects of color and how they effect us, and through education and experience in the fashion and color fields, I wrote my first book, "Your Name & Colors: Secret Keys to Your Beauty, Personality & Success!" Over the last ten years I have made many new discoveries. Through trial and error I discovered more practical and efficient ways to apply my color theories. In my second book, I will try to use God's spirit and color attributes in a more effective way. I hope you the readers will apply this to help in creating spiritual harmony along with all of the other basic applications of this theory (home-decor, wardrobe, career, financial, romance and personal decisions).

The letters in our names are attuned and vibrate to the different colors. We receive these different color-coded letter vibrations when we hear our names. I believe that these color vibrations enter our ears and are channeled through our inner ear cochlea gland that takes sound waves and turns them into nerve impulses. Then I believe these color vibrations are sent to the thalamus gland in our brain, (which I call the "grand central station" gland that takes in the information sent to the brain by the generally recognized human five senses of touch, taste, smell, sight and hearing). (There are some who believe we have seven senses). Then the thalamus registers and coordinates the information brought in by these senses and records them into our memory system, and how they affect different functions of our seven centers. In the following chapters, I will explain that the different letters and the sequence of the letters in your name will determine which colors are attuned to your seven energy centers. Therefore, laying the basic foundations of your talents, traits and color associations of these seven centers: (spiritual, mental, vocal, physical, control, emotional and sexual.)

The way that I believe these color vibrations are being carried is via the water in our mouth when we say a name and then through the water in our inner ear, brain, and throughout our bodies (it is well established that our bodies are composed of a great percentage of water). When is the only time you see a rainbow? When it rains, the water in the air is acting as a prism or refractor and carrier of the colors of sunlight. In the letter-color chart chapter you will learn how Sir Isaac Newton aligned the seven color spectrums to the "diatonic scale" (the musical scale). Scientist also have recently discovered that we have crystals in our inner ear which I believe could play a role in this color conversion and transportation in our inner ears. Another interesting fact is that our inner ear cochlea gland has three string tubes, or tuning bands, and there are three primary colors that can be separated and combined into the seven spectrums.

The reason why the majority of us cannot see these letter sounding colors entering our ears or vibrating in the air is because they are very subtle and short in length and impulse. The normal human eye see only colors that vibrate at 1/33 per second or 1/33,000 of an inch at the red end of the spectrum, and 1/67 per second or 1/67,000 of an inch at the violet end. Any other color impulses below this are invisible.

There are many things that we cannot see, feel, smell, taste, or hear that are in fact occurring, for example: have you ever been in a house with a dog that hears someone walking outside and you don't? Also, look how well animals can smell things from great distances that we cannot smell. These are simple examples that show when we don't notice things happening with our senses it does not mean they are not happening.

In a study done at a major university in California, forty -eight patients were told, while unconscious during surgery, to touch their ear. Thirty-three out of the forty-eight actually touched their ear, thus proving that our minds even while unconscious can still relay messages to our other body center parts from our different senses. This case happened to be a physical one relating to the sense of hearing.

"The skin's electrical activity changed remarkably when the ears heard words associated with emotion."- Carl Jung

If a medical team were to dissect a human body, would any of them be able to show us that person's spirit, emotions or mental thoughts? No, they would not. They could only show us bits and pieces of flesh, blood, muscles, fat, nerves and fluids; all physical substances. Yet we all know that humans have feelings and thoughts and this shows us that not all things that occur are always visible.

"The most beautiful thing we can experience is the mysterious. It is the source of all true art and science"- Albert Einstein

Let me also ask a question, which I have never been asked, other than by myself. If hearing our name affects our color associations and character traits, what about those that are deaf? At this time my answer is purely conjecture. First, as stated above, these color wavelengths are very subtle and invisible, so they could very well pass through the inner ear of a deaf person and still have an unconscious affect. Second we do not get all of our color wavelengths via our hearing. We have over two million cones and rods in our eye (this also brings into question those that are blind and their color associations) that take in color and relay them to our brain. We also take in light and color from skin absorption and through food (check chapter 17 for a list of the seven color spectrums in relation to the seven food color groups.

A German scientist, Dr. Anschutz, did much research in the area of color in relation to the deaf and blind. In his many pamphlets and books he states that many people connected each musical note with different tints and hues of color. He noted a very interesting case of an organist named Dorken, blind from the age of thirteen. He stated that this man, despite his blindness, could retain a very vivid memory of colors. Each note of the scale means for him a very different tint or hue. Each human voice produces a luminous vision-pleasant or otherwise. Each odor has its photism, every sensation such as muscular fatigue, toothache, even a bath, produces one. Sneezing brings it on. This sensitiveness would not seem to be a manifestation of disease.

Today there are what is called synesthesia organizations that claim to have thousands of documented cases of those that can see colors as people talk, taste colors of foods they eat, feel colors from touch, and other cross sense related experiences. I would only guess at this point in these cases of those that have synesthesia that there has been an abnormal cross wiring or fusion of cell walls in there thalamus gland, in their brain, possibly similar to when, changing radio stations, we pick up two different channels at once. Beethoven, Wagner, and many great musicians claimed to see colors emitting off of the different notes they played and Scriabin even made an organ which would light up different color tubes as he played it. Let me say at this point that if one is still skeptical of the "possibility" that these wavelength name/letter color vibrations are happening to us, then keep in mind radio, television, and all of the "wireless" cell phones and gadgets now a days. Are they not invisible and can television receive and project color? We should remember when the brilliant scientists were discovering the great inventions that we all know work and we use on a daily basis, such as airplanes, cars, cameras, computers, electrical appliances, radios, televisions. They were called "mad men", "so keep an open mind" because it is those that had an "open mind" that gave us all our wonderful modern conveniences.

NAME COLOROLOGY CAN BE USED TO:

~   Determine, and tune a person into their spiritual center colors, character traits, and talents which then can be used to determine, cultivate, and project your creative imaginative genius, spiritual moral conscience nature, youthful cheerful personality for your career, wardrobe, home-décor, and personal beauty applications.

~   Increase one's intellectual capabilities - (mental center), tune into your specific intellectual color and character traits, become more analytical, logical, and practical, to make good common sense decisions while projecting an intellectual image as well as for wardrobe, career, home-decor and personal use.

~   Tune into one's vocal colors, traits and talents for singing applications, harmonious wardrobe image, harmonious home-decor environment, organizing abilities and pleasant harmony interactions with others.

~   Determine your physical/heart center colors, traits and talents that stimulated you physically and expose your warm, kind, truthful, giving, heartfelt nature image and wardrobe, home-decor and career applications.

~   Learn your control/power center colors, traits and talents so you can project a dignified, refined, power business image, and stimulate your self-control empowerment nature to overcome all negative addictive habits and wardrobe, home-decor and career uses.

~   Find your emotional/ romantic soul center colors and personality character traits to project, and cultivate a romantic image along with use for personal romantic relationships, relaxing applications, and wardrobe, home-decor and career applications

~   Determine and enhance your sexual/glamorous/seductive/sensual personality character traits and colors for personal, wardrobe, home-decor and career uses.

~   Tune into any of your seven center colors to enhance your beauty and image

~ Stimulate and turn on your loved one romantically and sexually.

~ Learn how your name personality color vibration traits stimulate or conflict with loved ones or potential love mates, business partners or friends, and how you can use nicknames or change your name to make these relationships more compatible.

~ How to determine which centers are your strongest and which ones need to be cultivated and how to balance all your centers.

~ Determine your children's genius traits for career choices and what colors to use to decorate your children's rooms to help relax them and also stimulate their intellect.

In the near future I predict Name Colorology will be used by a vast amount of individuals, along with the following industries and career fields.

. Advertising	. Major Corporations
. Archeologists	. Marketing
. Artists	. Marriage Consultants
. Beauty Consultants	. Moral Consultants
. Cosmetologists	. Medical
. Career Consultants	. Modeling Agencies
. Dating Services	. Musical
. Designers	. Nutritionists
. Diplomats	. Parental Guidance
. Educational Institutions	. Photographers
. Entertainers	. Physiologists
. Endocrinologists	. Psychiatrists
. Fashion	. Relationship Consultants
. Financial	. Sales
. Governments	. Science
. Hospitals	. Sex therapist
. Historians	. Singers
. Image Consultants	. Spiritualist
. Interior Designers	. Sports Organizations
. Internet Industry	. Teachers
. Law	. Wardrobe Consultants
. Lawyers	. Writers
. Mail Order Industry	. Voice Instructors

I hope Name Colorology will bring physical scientists to work closer with spiritualists by using spiritual knowledge, which was divinely intended to help us to create a more harmonious world in which to live.

Here are some of the many compliments and testimonials which I have received after giving individual name/color readings.

~ What else is in your crystal ball?
~ That's exactly me.
~ That's so accurate, it's scary!
~ That makes sense, a lot of sense!
~ How did you know that?
~ How did you learn all this?
~ You know me better than I know myself!
~ You hit me to a "T".

TESTIMONIALS:

"This man has an amazing talent. The phones were hot, very hot!" (Al Kline- Host of the Kelly and Kline show, X-100 FM, San Francisco, Ca.)

"A wonderful guest-- He seems right on. I am very fascinated by this philosophy. I've got to read this book." (Ricky Rafner, host of the Ricky Rafner Show, KVON, Napa, Ca.)

"Colors can make or break your appearance and enhance your success. Mr. Greycastle has the color magic to sparkle, color-up, and brighten your life--day and night. He can guide you to superb perfection and color harmony." (Patricia Bragg, Ph.D., Author, Nutritionist to the Stars, Santa Barbara, Ca.)

"To apply his theory, not only a spectacular result can be achieved in the home, but it could become an environment that enables that client to achieve their dreams--creative, financial, romantic, etc. I plan to use it! (Peggy Abbott, Interior designer, Benicia, Ca.)

"Genius, pure genius". Mr. Greycastles' only problem is that he is so far ahead of the crowd it will take time for others to catch up. I predict he will eventually be recognized as the "Color and Fashion King"! Conroy Stillman, Owner Stillman Styles.

"Thank you for the consultation on my interview with the hospital. By using key words, which you gave me, in my interview I received immediate acceptance. Both women were nodding their heads yes to all my answers. The interview went extremely smooth and I left on a very positive note. They did caution me that it might be three weeks before I heard from personnel--but to my surprise, I was called the next week. Knowing what each women was looking for in conversation was extremely effective in guiding the interview to a successful result." Nancy Juliene Frazier

"Thank you for the wonderful presentation of, "Your name and Colors". The ladies enjoyed your class so much that each and everyone called me the next day to say how very much they did

enjoy the class and how very helpful and kind you were to them. So many thanks from all of us."
Joy Boles-Letang, The Hypnotherapy Center Dublin, Ca.

I finally know, "My Colors, Styles and Natural Creative Traits", I even know what colors to decorate my home in, thanks to Mr. Greycastle, I received a lot more than I had anticipated, what an interesting person! Henriet Reynolds - Professional Cosmetologist - 28 years

I foresee in the near future when highly sensitive electromagnetic visual and audio equipment will be able to tune into a persons vibrational tone and color wave length in any of their seven energy centers to help them spiritually, mentally, vocally, physically, control, emotionally and sexually. I believe there is a strong possibility that Name Colorology will eventually create a whole new medical field. It will possibly blend psychology and psychiatry with endocrinology and be called endocrine psychology and endocrine psychiatry.

Name Colorology will possibly be routinely used to:

~ Control addictive and compulsive habits.
~ Relax those under stress.
~ Increase workers creativity and productivity.
~ Cultivate children's genius.
~ Produce smarter, more productive and socially adaptive students.
~ Increase financial and scientific productivity by business and governments.
~ Create color environments with paint colors that are attuned to individual personality traits.

Name Colorology will unlock many secrets to the human personality code and answer questions such as why.

~ Some people are more harmonious and others are not.
~ Certain individuals are successful financially and others fail financially.
~ Some people are good singers and others are not.
~ Certain people are creative and others not so creative.

Name Colorology will become the leading philosophy of the beauty, cosmetic, interior decorating and fashion fields.

In the very near future we here at the Name Colorology Group will be developing a whole new industry of products and services directly related to our philosophy. These will be available at our internet site www.namecolorology.com and will also be offered through are toll free 1-877-505-9100 telephone number, direct mail, catalogs, and proposed magazine and television infomercials. (For those who would like to join our affiliate program and be paid an excellent percentage fee for sales made by affiliate referrals, come to our web site and we will provide information on how you can become an affiliate. We plan to eventually be offering the following:

~ Audio Tapes
~ Bath Salts
~ Beauty Products
~ Books
~ Business Sales Productivity Training
(For Increasing Sales)
~ Candles
~ Calendars (of home interiors, lingerie, swimsuits, etc.)
~ Career Consulting
~ Color Charts (for wardrobe, home-decor and career)
~ Color Fans (with a far greater amount of colors that list the character attributes that are attuned to the different tints, true hue and shades of all the colors
~ Cosmetics
~ Custom Made Wardrobe Designs for Gala Events and Other Occasions (this service is available now)
~ Ebooks (for those who want to download our books electronically)
~ E-mail Consulting
~ Fabrics
~ Image Consulting

~ Interior Design/Consulting
~ Job Interview Consulting
(It is very important to analyze your interviewers name)
~ Lingerie'
~ Magazine
~ Mail Order Catalogs
~ Models
~ Name Compatibility Consulting
(for romantic relationships etc.)
~ Naming Babies
~ Naming Pets
~ Nutritional Products
(especially attuned to the
7 energy centers)
~ Paints (that will be attuned and listing the character attributes to all the colors)
~ Perfumes
~ Personal Consultation Service
~ Ready to Wear Fashion Line Catalog
~ Retail Stores
~ Soaps
~ Telephone Consultations
~ Training Seminars
~ Wardrobe Consulting
~ Video Tapes

Chapter 1

THE SEVEN CENTERS/CHAKRA S CENTERS/ENDOCRINE GLANDS

Seven Energy Centers

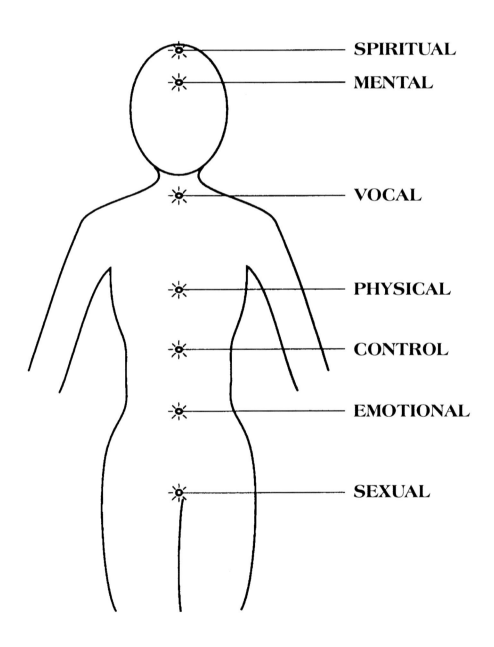

SPIRITUAL

MENTAL

VOCAL

PHYSICAL

CONTROL

EMOTIONAL

SEXUAL

Seven Chakra Centers

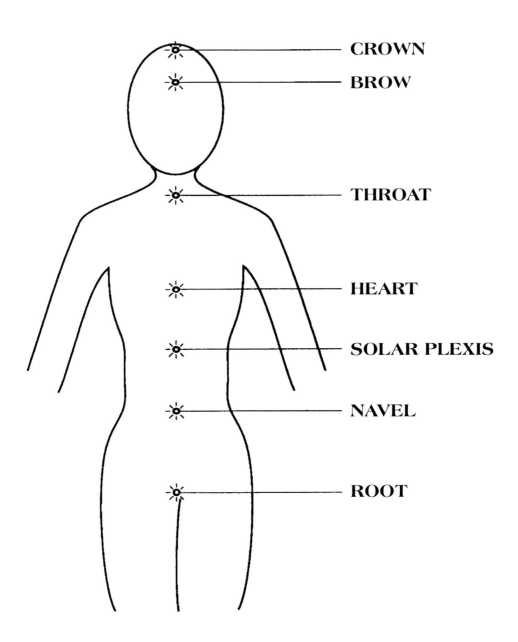

CROWN

BROW

THROAT

HEART

SOLAR PLEXIS

NAVEL

ROOT

Seven Endocrine Glands

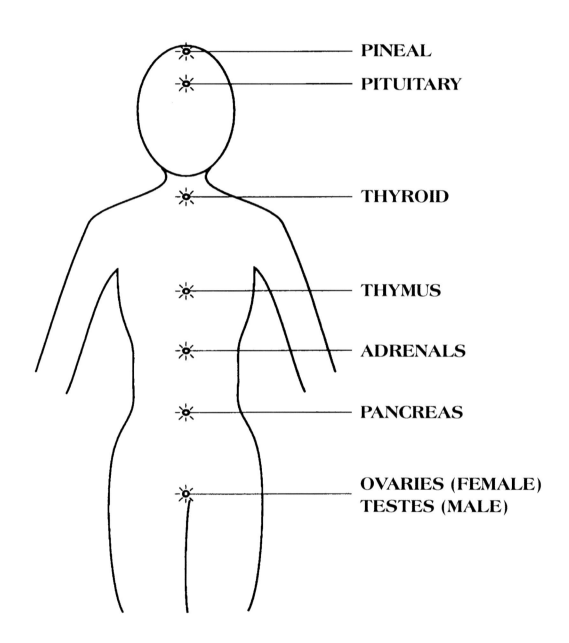

PINEAL

PITUITARY

THYROID

THYMUS

ADRENALS

PANCREAS

OVARIES (FEMALE)
TESTES (MALE)

SEVEN IMAGE TYPES & VARIATIONS OF THESE TYPES

Spiritual- spiritual/moral, youthful/wholesome, sporty/cheerful, creative/imaginative & inventive/genius

Mental- intellectual/studious, analytical/logical & practical/non-flashy

Vocal- harmonious/pleasant, neat/organized & fluent/talkative

Physical- warm/affectionate, honest/sincere, forgiving/compassionate, kind/giving, physical/dramatic

Control- empowered/in-control, authoritative/corporate, dignified/regal, refined/cultured & formal/serious

Emotional- romantic/soulful, soft/feminine, relaxed/restful & content/emotional

Sexual- sexy/glamorous, earthy/seductive, secretive/mysterious & grounded/survivalist

In the future we will be explaining how to use our system to create hundreds of combination image types using your center colors.

We know all of us need new and better ways to give ourselves the edge or advantage to make the difference between success and failure. We here at Name Colorology Group offer several new tools in which to achieve these goals. You can call 1-877-505-9100 or contact us at our web site www.namecolorology.com any time for consultation for help in this field of expertise.

For those interested we presently offer by phone and e-mail: wardrobe, home-decor and career color/design service.

Chapter 2

THE SEVEN COLOR SPECTRUMS
AND THEIR CHARACTER ATTRIBUTES

In this chapter you will learn the character attributes of the seven color spectrums: flesh, purple, red, orange, yellow, green and blue. In the following chapters you will learn which colors are attuned to your different energy centers: spiritual, mental, vocal, physical, control, emotional and sexual, and how these colors affect and determine your character traits, talents and color associations.

THE FLESH SPECTRUM

The flesh spectrum ranges from the whites, beige's, tans, light browns, browns, dark browns, and dark chocolate browns. The letters that are attuned to the flesh spectrum are A, H, O and V sounding letters. God's character attributes of the flesh spectrum are: articulateness, cleanliness, compensation, coordination, harmony, introspective, memory recall, morality, organization, practicality, perception, unity (mind-body-soul), and universality. In the following center chapters you will find out which of your centers are attuned to the flesh spectrum. If you have cultivated God's positive character traits listed above these will be your traits and talents of any of the centers attuned to this spectrum. If you have not cultivated his positive traits of this spectrum and cultivated the negative traits of this spectrum you will have the following traits: confusion, disorderliness, filthiness, forgetfulness, immorality, idolatry, inarticulateness, inconsiderateness, inconsistency, lacking coordination, inharmonious and impractical.

THE PURPLE SPECTRUM

The purple spectrum colors range from light lavenders, true hue purple, and deep violets. The letters that are attuned to the purple spectrum are B, I, P, and W, sounding letters. God's positive character traits of this spectrum are: civilized, cultured, dedicated, detailed, dignified, empowered, idealistic, intuitive, loyal, mature, regal, self sacrificing, and tasteful. The negative traits are domination, fanaticism, lack of taste, monopolization, pettiness, pompousness, snobbishness, superiority, treachery, uncivilized, undignified, and lacking loyalty.

THE RED SPECTRUM

The red spectrum ranges from pink reds, rose reds, true hue red, cranberry reds, and dark wine reds. The letters that are attuned to this spectrum are C, J, Q, and X sounding letters. God's positive character attributes of the red spectrum are: beauty of manner (elegance), benevolence (sense of good will), charitableness, chivalry, compassion, courteous (mercifulness), gracefulness, gratefulness (thankfulness), honesty (sincerity), persistence (tenaciousness), physical life energy, romance, and valor (courage). The negative traits of the red spectrum are: brutality, dishonesty, excessive carnal desire, impulsiveness (impatience), jealousy (envy), physical egotism, physical laziness, pitilessness (lack of compassion), rudeness (coarseness), savageness (barbaric).

THE ORANGE SPECTRUM

The orange spectrum ranges from the light peaches, light corals, true hue orange, rust, and dark earthy rust oranges. The letters that are attuned to this spectrum are D, K, R and Y sounding letters. God's positive character traits of the orange spectrum are: affection (fondness), creativity, inspirational enthusiasm, joyfulness, kindness (warm heartedness), repentance, self-assurance, speculation, venturesome, and versatility. The negative traits are: boastfulness, despair (depression), destructiveness, exhibitionism, flamboyance, and unpleasantness.

THE YELLOW SPECTRUM

The yellow spectrum consists of the light pale yellows, true hue yellow, gold yellows, and dark copper yellows. The letters that are attuned to this spectrum are E, L, S and Z sounding letters. God's positive yellow traits are: analytical, cheerfulness, clarity, comprehension, decisiveness, friendliness, glorification (of God), intellectual, logic, optimism (positive thinking), and reasonableness. The negative character traits: conniving, deceit, pessimism, shrewdness and vindictiveness.

THE GREEN SPECTRUM

The green spectrum ranges from light mint green, true hue green, to dark forest green. The letters that are attuned to this spectrum are F, M and T sounding letters. God's positive attributes are: balance, caution, control (self-control), cooperation, critical discrimination, equitableness (agreeableness), impartiality (fairness), lawfulness, peacefulness, and poise. The negative traits are: bias, callousness, disagreeableness, envy, lack of judgment, miserliness, sense of injustice, and suspicion.

THE BLUE SPECTRUM

The blue spectrum ranges from light baby blues, sky blues, true hue blue, royal blues, navy blues, and dark midnight blues. The letters that are attuned to this spectrum are G, N and U sounding letters. Blue is the color of the spiritual, celestial, ethereal universe. God's positive blue traits are: inventive, dependability, diplomacy (tactfulness), discretion, dutifulness, faithfulness, fluid, meditative, natural sense of beauty, open-mindedness, serenity, social, soothing, soulful, spacious, spirited, style, suave, and tactful. The negative traits are: apathy, closed mindedness, coldness, distrust, indiscretion, lack of faith, lack of spirit, laziness, superstitious, undependable, and tactlessness.

THE WHITE SPECTRUM

Spiritual - Giving - Healing

White is a Spiritual color of the Holy Trinity, the Father, Son (Christ light), And Holy Ghost. It is God's anti-gravitational color; the color of purity, giving, cleansing, healing and protection. To cultivate the characteristics of white is to become more spiritual and closer to God, and to shed the dark trappings of sin and materialism. White light reflects 98% light and consumes 2%. Therefore it allows us to see in its presence. When we want to uplift our spirits we need to bring white light into our lives. We need to escape the dark trappings of too much gravitational earth-iness. All light colors in the different spectrums have white added to them. Interior decorators use white in colors to add brightness, cheer, cleanliness, spaciousness and spirit. It is the ener-gizing color. It is a wonderful protective color. White is active and positive. Wear white after you go through a spiritual healing and see how good it feels on you. White light is very unfolding and giving and awakens our higher spiritual selves. Those that have cultivated the traits of white are very giving, healing, pure, spiritual, wholesome and close to God.

THE GRAY SPECTRUM

Mutual Agreement - Neutrality - Separator

The gray spectrum ranges from light silver to dark ash grays. Gray is achieved by mixing white with black. White (spiritual and giving), and black (earthy and consuming). Gray is the color of neutrality, neither aggressive or backing up, gray stands its neutral ground. Gray is mutual agreement, giving and taking. Gray is like a prism or mist from which rain allows sunlight to be separated into a rainbow of individual colors. Therefore gray has the ability to separate the con-tents of elements into their true hues and character. Those that have all of the 7 colors in their names are gray, emotional people, so gray people will be emotionally giving and taking, not real-ly wanting to take sides in matters, seeing both sides. They give back to others emotionally what has been given to them. They have a natural ability to expose and separate the facts into their particular categories. If you compliment a gray emotional person they will compliment you back. If you help them they will help you back. If you don't, they won't. If you're kind to them they will be kind to you. Gray people are like mirrors; they reflect back just what they see. If one wants to tone down colors if they feel a color is too bright, bold, or strong, then they should mix a little gray with them to mellow them or render them a bit more neutral. Gray has a relaxing, neutralizing affect for those that need to tone down their feelings, or who get too overly involved in too many emotional situations. Gray people make good diplomats, judges and negotiators. Fields were there is a need to limit strong emotions.

GRAY SAYINGS:

Giving and taking the mutual agreement that makes marriage a delight. - D.G. Rolliet

When in the act of investigating, make sure first, to divorce your prejudices from the investigation in order to get the accurate facts, then fair judgment can be made. - D.G. Rolliet

THE BLACK SPECTRUM

Consuming - Firm Commitment - New Beginnings - Rest

Black is the color of consuming, it consumes or absorbs 98% light and reflects 2%; the opposite of white. Black is secretive (hidden). Black pulls in. It is very gravitational, earthy and heavy. It is secretive and seductive in nature, that is how the saying, " the little sexy black dress," came about. Black is firm in commitment (serious commitment). Priests choose black for their habits as a symbol of firm commitment to God and celibacy. Black is new beginnings, the ending of a cycle and the beginning of a new one. God gave us the darkness of night in which to conserve our energies, rest, and regenerate ourselves so that when the light of dawn comes we will be ready to use this energy for our daily work in the light of day. We should use black when we want to conserve our energies. Black is also excellent color for listening when we want to consume what others are saying. The negative traits of black are: anti-God, anti-spiritual (no spiritual belief), excessive anger, too firm in opinion, too earthy or macho, and dark trappings of sin.

Chapter 3

ANALYZING YOUR NAME CORRECTLY

In this Chapter, and the following seven center chapters (spiritual, mental, vocal, physical, control, emotional and sexual), you will learn how the different letters in your name are attuned to the seven colors. Depending where those letter/colors are positioned in your name will determine what colors are attuned to your seven energy centers. Once you have determined your center colors, you will then be able to know your personality character traits, talents and color associations for wardrobe, home-decor, career choices, relationships and other personal applications. You may find that you have a certain color attuned to more than one center.

The very first step in determining your letter colors of your name is first determining your "real name". What I mean by real name is the name that you are called by most people, for example, if your official name is Robert, but everyone calls you Bob, then you would use "Bob" as your real name. You also have to consider nicknames, for example, if your official name were Patricia, yet everyone called you "Patty" you would have to analyze your name as Patty. If you are called both your official given name and a nickname on an equal basis you would then analyze both of them. You also must consider if you have children that call you dad, daddy, pop, mother, mommy, mom, etc., on a regular basis. These names must also be included in your full name analysis. One other name situation some must consider, is if you have a title included in your name for example if you are a Doctor, or Mister etc., that you are called on a regular basis.

You will also learn how to analyze the correct phonetic letter sounds in your name and to find what colors are attuned to your seven centers **(this is an absolute must in order to analyze your name and colors correctly)**.

Let us give you some example names of what we mean by correct phonetic sounding letters:

~ Eileen is actually pronounced   (I-len). The first (E) is silent and the third (e) is silent
~ Cynthia is pronounced   (Sin-the-a).   (C) sounds as (S) and (y) sounds to (i) & 2nd (i) to (e)
~ Carol is pronounced (Kar-ol). The (C) sounds to (K)
~ Jimmy is actually pronounced (Jim-m-e). (y) sounds to (e)

You also must take into consideration the pronunciation of foreign names such as:

~ Julio is phonetically pronounced (Hu-le-o). (J) sounds to (H) and the (i) to (e)
~ Jaunita is pronounced (Wa-ne-da). (J) sounds to (W) (u) is silent (i) to (e) (t) to (d)

One more rule in analyzing a name is the actual speed that it is normally pronounced.

~ Betty- At normal speed is pronounced   (Bed-d). t's actually sound to (d)
~ Dennis- At normal speed is pronounced (Den-as). 2nd (n) is silent and (i) sounds to soft (a)

If you have any problem analyzing your name we highly advise a Name Colorology Consultant to analyze your name in detail. We have very reasonable consultation fees through our toll free 1-877-505-9100 or our web site e-mail at namecolorology.com. Go to chapter 36 which lists our service and product prices. You can also find out about any updated info, new products, future products, or events.

We highly recommend that any person interested in getting an accurate detailed reading of a name use one of our experienced professional analyzers at least one time.

As you determine the colors of your seven centers and their character traits, after each center chapter, then go to the back of the book and fill in your three-part chart for wardrobe, home-décor, and career choices.

We advise that you read about all the center color types so you will be able to understand others (your children, family, friends and business associates, etc.). You will also see how all of the different color types dominate certain fields. For example: 70% of the most famous writers are purple spiritual people, the majority of the most famous and successful architects, lawyers, models and peace makers are green spiritual people, and 70% or more of the most famous singers are orange vocal center people and many more such examples. You will also learn how to acquire new or different color traits to different centers for improvement in certain skills for your career and creative choices.

Read our theory following the color center chapters about the possibility of hormonal center addiction along with balancing all of your centers, and how you could possibly use this theory to control and defeat your negative addictions and habits.

THE LETTER-COLOR CODE

In the late 17th century Sir Isaac Newton announced his discovery of how sunlight, white light, could be separated into the seven colors of the spectrum by way of the prism. This is fairly well known, but Newton also aligned (attuned), the seven colors to the "Diatonic Scale", the musical scale; A to indigo, B to purple, C to red, D to orange, E to yellow, F to green and G to blue. I have changed the (A) to indigo, to the flesh color spectrum, off white, beiges, tans, light browns, browns, dark browns and dark chocolate browns (some refer to these colors as the earth colors). The reason I aligned (A) to flesh verses indigo is because I believe Newton was referring to the flesh colors when he was saying indigo. There are four primary reasons why I believe my changing of indigo to flesh is correct.

One: In the days of Newton scientist and chemist use to mix certain chemical acids with the deep blue/violet dye of the indigo plant which actually produced a copper flesh color (similar to the color of a persons skin when they get a copper suntan). If you were to refer to very old dictionaries when looking up the word indigo you would also find descriptions of brown indigo, copper indigo and flesh indigo.

Two: There are 3 primary colors, red, yellow and blue, along with four secondary colors. When you mix the red primary with the yellow primary you get orange, one of the secondary colors. When you mix red with blue you get purple, the second secondary color. When you mix yellow with blue you get green, the third secondary color. So now, the only other way of mixing your primary colors together to make the fourth secondary color would be to mix all three primary colors, red, yellow, and blue at the same time. When you do this you will see that it produces a flesh color and not an indigo blue/purple color, therefore making flesh the 7th color spectrum. Mixing blue/purple indigo is not following the above mixing formulas because blue has already been mixed with red to produce purple. So, all one would be doing to get this blue purple is just mixing some more blue with it, which as I say does not follow the formula of just mixing primaries together to get a secondary.

Three: In interviewing thousands of individuals whom I describe as being flesh spiritual center people, whose first or last name start with A, H, O or V, overwhelmingly pick the flesh spectrum colors as their favorites.

Four: As you will find out after learning the character traits of the different colors you will find, yellow as the mental color, red as the physical color, blue the spirit and soul color. Mix the three together and the spiritual character meaning adds up to that old saying, "Mind, Body and Spirit", or some say "Mind, Body and Soul", which can be also interpreted as Harmony. Again in my many interviews with flesh spiritual people they overwhelmingly stress a desire to have cleanliness, harmony, morality, music organization; all key flesh spectrum character traits in their lives.

All things that are alive vibrate a wavelength and an aura: humans, animals, plants, insects and sounds. Here is the color alphabet that aligns, attunes, the entire wave length vibrations of the letters of the alphabet to the seven colors.

LETTER COLOR CHART

Flesh	Purple	Red	Orange	Yellow	Green	Blue
A	B	C	D	E	F	G
H	I	J	K	L	M	N
O	P	Q	R	S	T	U
V	W	X	Y	Z		

Chapter 4

YOUR SPIRITUAL/YOUTHFUL/
GENIUS CENTER COLORS, TRAITS AND TALENTS

Spiritual Center
Top and Middle of Head

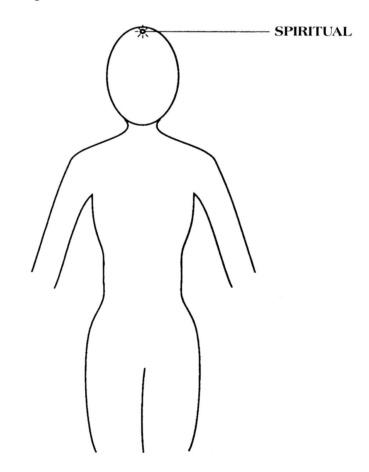

Your spiritual center is located at the crown of your head, in the area of your pineal gland, and the area which eastern philosophies call the crown chakra, it has basically 3 or 4 functions. It is where your moral conscience of right and wrong originates. Also it is where your ability to believe in Gods spiritual world and to have faith and optimism that things will work out in your life in troublesome times if you follow his teachings. It is also our youthful, wholesome, happy, cheerful, energy center, and is also where your creative imagination genius originates.

Your spiritual center colors will look and feel spiritual, moral, wholesome, clean, happy, cheerful, creative and imaginative on and around you. In this world we live in today, I feel that the majority have bypassed and neglected their spiritual center and have not chosen to cultivate it. That is why we live in such an immoral world, nowadays man has forgot about his spiritual higher self and decided to cultivate his lower earthy mental center without first consulting his higher spirit mind. In other words, "He has no conscience." History has shown us many tyrants who stole, killed, and maimed millions of people to obtain their earthy material goals. If a person would first consult their higher spiritual mind for the right decisions and get in the habit of acting off of this center than they would not make these horrendous mistakes. History has shown us those that have cultivated their spiritual centers such as Jesus and all the saints, popes, priests, nuns, monks and other spiritually enlightened people, who have contributed to others in need such as Gandhi and Mother Theresa.

If everyone would take it upon himself or herself to cultivate their higher spiritual self just a little bit more, then the world would be a lot better place to live in.

The spiritual center is also what I call the supreme optimism center and the faith center, when we use or hear sayings such as: "Just do what you feel is right and things will work out," or, "Just have faith, things will eventually work themselves out." What we are doing is trying to stimulate our higher spiritual mind which controls our ability to have faith which sends a message to our lower earthy mind to relax and stop worrying about a problem it is having trouble handling. It's like a cool breeze on a hot night when things seem unbearable.

A good way to uplift ones spirit is to laugh even if it is a forced, phony (ha-ha) laugh; just keep doing it until you break into a genuine laugh. Laughing has a vibrating effect, just as a jackhammer or vibrating drill, and breaks up solid, hard, or bad feelings. Sometimes I do this myself when I get in bad moods or my temper is starting to boil, and it helps to change my mood almost instantly. It also makes me feel ten years younger. How can you tell if you're a spiritual type? Spiritual types usually are the people that have a youthful, spirited, wholesome smile on their face. They also tend to believe in the spiritual world, are very religious, and are usually very kind and concerned about the well being of others. They are also very imaginative and creative.

"Imagination is more important than knowledge"- Albert Einstein

The letters in your name that determine your spiritual center color traits and talents are the first sounding letters in your first name, your middle name only if you are called by it, and your last name. For example: the name (B)randy (J)ones, looking at the letter- color chart on page 25 you will see that this is a purple and red spiritual center person. This person would then go to the purple and red spiritual center color chapters to learn about their spiritual center color traits and talents. If both the first and last name spiritual center color letters are the same, then it

27

would make a double spiritual center color person. For example: (B)randy (B)aker is a double purple spiritual center person. After you have read about your spiritual center traits and talents go to the color fan in the photo color section and determine your precise spiritual center colors. After you have done all of the above go to the three-part chart in the back of the book and record your spiritual center colors. Use your spiritual center colors in bright, clean, creative, wholesome, youthful types of materials and prints. To learn the basic steps to cultivate your spiritual center go to chapter 28.

FLESH SPECTRUM SPIRITUAL CENTER PEOPLE

Flesh spectrum spiritual center people are those whose first, middle only if used, or last name start with an A, H, O or V sounding letter. The flesh spectrum positive character traits are: articulateness, cleanliness, compensation, coordination, harmony, introspective, memory recall, morality, organization practicality, perception, unity, mind-body-soul, and universality.

Flesh spiritual people need and want cleanliness, harmony, music, neatness and organization in their lives. They are usually very giving, moral, and harmonious people. They also have excellent memory and organizational abilities.

The negative character traits of flesh spiritual people are: confusion, disorderliness, filthiness, forgetfulness, idolatry, immorality, impractical, inarticulate, inconsiderateness, inconsistency, inharmonious and lacking coordination. The flesh spectrum ranges from the whites, beiges, tans, light browns, browns, dark browns, and dark chocolate browns. Your favorite flesh spiritual center colors will look and feel very cheerful, clean, creative, happy, imaginative, moral, spacious, spirited and wholesome on and around you. Use your spiritual center colors to create these images and feelings in your wardrobe and home-decor. Go to the color fans in the photo section of the book and determine your favorite flesh spiritual center colors then go to the 3-part chart in the back of the book and record them.

NATURAL CAREER FIELDS THAT FLESH SPIRITUAL PEOPLE EXCEL IN:

Accountants
Archeologists/Anthropologists
Cosmetologists/ skin experts
Financial Advisers
Geologists
Money Managers
Moral Advisers/Religious leaders
Musical Composers
Organizers
Paleontologists
Time Management Consultants

Flesh Spectrum - Harmony - History - Music- Organization
(A, H, O, V)
Some W's sound to V
Flesh Spiritual Center
Anthropologists - Archeologists - Dendrochronologists- Geologists - Paleontologists

(A)braham Gottlob (W)erner
(A)lan Dundes
(A)lessandro Duranti
(A)lfred (V)incent Kidder
(A)lfred Lothar (W)egener
(A)ndrew Douglass
(A)nna (H)adwick Gayton
(A)ntoine Yves Gogriet

(A)rthur (A) Demarest
George Clapp (V)abillant
(H)arold Gladwin
(H)eimich Schliemann
(H)iram Bigham
(H)oward Carter
Jack (H)orner
James (H)utton

Kenneth Page (O)akley
Louis (A)gassiz
Luis Walter (A)lvarez
Sir (A)lan Gardiner
Sir (A)rthur John Evans
(V)era Mae Green
(V)ere Gordon Childe
William (H)enry (H)olmes

Flesh Spiritual Center
Musicial Arrangers and Artists

(A)aron Copeland
(A)bbe Lane
(A)be Most
(A)dolph Green
(A)ileen Stanley
(A)J Mclean
(A)laddin Pallante
(A)lan Dale
(A)lan De Witt
(A)lanis Morisette
(A)lan Jackson
(A)lan Menken
(A)lannah Myles
(A)lan Parson
(A)lberta (H)unter
(A)ldridge Sisters
(A)lexander Nikolaievich
Scriabin
(A)lex North
(A)l Green
(A)l (H)ibbler
(A)l (H)irt
(A)licia Keys
(A)lison Krauss
(A)l Jardine
(A)l Jarreau
(A)l Jolsen
(A)llen Toussaint
(A)llie Wrubel
(A)l Martino

(A)l Menke
(A)l Nobel
(A)l Plant
(A)l Rinker
(A)l Stewart
(A)madeus Mozart
(A)my (A)rnell
(A)my Grant
(A)na Barbara
(A)na Cani
(A)ndre Previn
(A)ndrea Bocelli
(A)ndrea Gruber
(A)ndrea Segovia
(A)ndrew Lloyd Webber
(A)ndrew Sisters
(A)ndy Gibb
(A)ndy Kim
(A)ndy Parrtridge
(A)ndy Russell
(A)ndy Williams
(A)ngelo Moore
(A)ni Difranco
(A)nita Baker
(A)nita Boyer
(A)nita (O)day
(A)nita Ward
(A)nn Miller
(A)nnabelle Graham
(A)nne Murray

(A)nnette Funicello
(A)nnie Lennox
(A)nn Richards
(A)nton Dvorak
(A)ntonio (V)ivaldi
(A)ntonio Stradivarius
(A)nton Karas
(A)ntonyo Dontonyo
(A)retha Franklin
(A)rnie (H)aines
(A)rt Depew
(A)rt Garfunkel
(A)rthur Duncan
(A)rthur Lyman
(A)rthur Murry
(A)rthur Rubenstein
(A)rthur Wright
(A)rt Jarrett
(A)rt Lund
(A)va Barber
Barbara (A)nne (H)awkins
Barbara (H)endricks
Bertie (H)iggins
Betty (V)an
Bill (A)nderson
Bill (H)aley
Billie (H)olliday
Billy (V)aughn
Billy (V)era
Birtie (H)iggins

Bob (A)llen
Bobby (H)atfield
Bobby (H)ebb
Bobby (V)ee
Bobby (V)inton
Bob (H)aymes
Bob (H)aywood
Bob (H)ouston
Bryan (A)brams
Buck (O)wens
Buddy (H)olly
Buddy (H)ughes
Cannonball (A)dderley
Chet (A)tkins
Chrissie (H)ynde
Christina (A)guilera
Claire (H)ogan
Connie (H)aines
Corey (H)art
Dan (H)ill
Darren (H)ayes
Daryl (H)all
David (A)llyn
David (O)istrakh
Debra (H)arry
Dick (H)arding
Dick (H)aynes
Dick (H)yman
Dolores Dodie (O)Neill
Dolores (H)awkins
Don (H)artman
Dorsey (A)nderson
Dorothy (A)llen
Eddie (A)rnold
Eddie (H)aywood
Eddie (H)olland
Eddie (H)oward
Edward (H)eyman
Edwin (H)awkins
Elvis (A)aron Presley
Emmy Lou (H)arris
Ernestine (A)nderson
Faith (H)ill
Ferlin (H)usky
Francis (H)unt
Frank (A)lbert Sinatra
Frankie (A)valon
Franki (V)alli

Fred (A)staire
Gene (H)oward
Gene (V)incent
George (H)amilton
Gilbert (O)'Sullivan
Glen (H)ughes
Gloria (H)art
Gloria (V)an
Grayson (H)unter
Guispe (V)erde
Guy (H)ovis
(H)al Derwin
(H)ank Locklin
(H)ank Williams
(H)ank Williams, Jr.
(H)arlan (H)oward
(H)arold (A)rlen
(H)arold Melvin
(H)arriet (H)illiard
(H)arry Babbitt
(H)arry Bellafonte
(H)arry Brooks
(H)arry Burns
(H)arry Chapin
(H)arry Cool
(H)arry Connick Jr.
(H)arry Mills
(H)arry Nilsson
(H)arry Richmond
(H)arry Wayne Cacye
(H)elen Forrest
(H)elen (H)umes
(H)elen Lee
(H)elen (O)'Connell
(H)elen Reddy
(H)elen Southern
(H)elen Ward
(H)enry Cuesta
(H)enry Mancini
(H)erb (A)lbert
(H)erbert Blumstedt
(H)erb Fame
(H)erbie (H)ancock
(H)erb Magidson
(H)erb Mills
(H)orst Jankowski
(H)oward (A)shman
(H)oward Dulanny

(H)oward Goodman
(H)oward Keel
(H)owie Dorough
(H)uddie Leadbetter
(H)ugh Martin
(H)ugh Maseakla
(H)ugo Friedhoper
(H)ugo Winterhalter
India .(A)rie
Isaac (H)ayes
Ivie (A)nderson
Jackie (H)orne
Jack (H)askell
Jack (H)unter
Jake (H)ess
Jane (H)arvey
Jeff (H)ealey
Jerry (V)ale
Jessica (A)ndrews
Jimmy (H)endrix
Jo (A)nn Greer
John Lee (H)ooker
John (O)ates
Johnny (H)orton
Jon (A)nderson
Julie (A)ndrews
June (H)utton
Karrin (A)llyson
Kay (A)llen
Kitty (A)llen
Kristin (H)ersh
Larry (H)opper
Lauryn (H)ill
Lazy Bill (H)uggins
Lena (H)orne
Leroy (A)nderson
Leroy (V)anDyke
Louanne (H)ogan
Louis (A)rmstrong
Ludwig (V)on Beethoven
Luther (V)andross
Lyn (A)nderson
Lynn (A)nderson
Marie (H)utton
Marie (O)smond
Marilyn (H)orne
Marion (H)utton
Marjorie (H)ughes

Martha (V)andella
Marvin (H)amlisch
Maxium (V)engerov
Merle (H)aggart
Micheal (A)uthor
Michael (O)'Brien
Micheal (H)utchence
Mike (O)ldfield
Mr. (A)ker Bilk
Nancy (H)arrow
(O)leta (A)dams
(O)liver
(O)livia Newton John
(O)scar (H)ammerstein
(O)smond Family
(O)tis Blackwell
(O)tis Redding
(O)tis Williams
Paul (A)nka
Paula (A)bdul
Paul (H)armon

Patti (A)ustin
Ray (A)nthony
Ray (H)endricks
Rex (H)arrison
Richard (H)ayman
Richard (W)agner-
  pronounced V
Richie (V)alens
Ric (O)lasek
Ron (A)nderson
Roy (O)rbison
Ruthie (V)ale
Sally (A)nn (H)arris
Sarah (V)aughan
Shirley (H)orn
Terry (A)llen
Toni (A)rden
Toni (A)ubin
Tori (A)mos
Trace (A)dkins
Ty (H)erndon
(V)an Clyeburn
(V)an (H)alen
(V)an (H)eusen
(V)an Morrison
(V)anessa Williams
(V)eronique Gens
(V)esta Goodman

(V)ickie Joyce
(V)ickie Sue Robinson
(V)icki Spencer
(V)icky Lawrence
(V)ictor Borge
(V)ictor Damone
(V)ictor Young
(V)ikki Carr
(V)ince Gill
(V)ince Guaraldi
(V)ince Martell
(V)irginia (H)ayes
(V)irginia Maxey
(V)irginia Rodriguez
(V)ladamir (H)orowitz
(V)on Trapp Family
Whitney (H)ouston
Wilber (H)arrison
Woody (H)erman

Famous Flesh Spiritual Center Cosmetologists, Make-Up Artists and Skin Care Experts

(A)ubrey (H)ampton
(A)drian (A)rpell
Dr. (A)lfonso Di Mino
Elizabeth (A)rden
Forrest (A)kerman
(H)elene Rene
(H)elene Rubinstein
Kevin (A)ucion
Lee (H)arman
(V)ictoria Raynor
(V)incent Kehoe

SAYINGS THAT STIMULATE FLESH SPIRITUAL PEOPLE:

Order is a lovely nymph, the child of beauty and wisdom; her attendants are comfort, neatness, and activity; her abode is the valley of happiness; she is always to be found when sought for, and never appears so lovely as when contrasted with her opponent, disorder. - Johnson

We do not keep the outward form of order, where there is deep disorder in the mind. - Shakespeare

Order is heaven's first law. - Pope

He who has no taste for order, will often wrong in his judgment, and seldom considerate or conscientious in his actions. - Lavater

Order is the sanity of the mind, the health of the body, the peace of the city, the security of the state. - As the beams to a house, as the bones to the body, so is order to all things. - Southey

The heavens themselves, the planets, and his center, observe degree, priority and place, insisture, course, proportion, season, form, office, and custom in all line of order. - Shakespeare

Have a time and place for everything, and do everything in its time and place, and you will not only accomplish more, but have far more leisure than those who are always hurrying, as if vainly attempting to overtake time that had been lost. - Tryon Edwards

PURPLE SPIRITUAL PEOPLE

Purple spiritual people are those whose first, middle if used routinely, or last names start with B, I, P, or W sounding letters. Purple spiritual people, when cultivating and operating off of God's positive purple character attributes, are civilized, cultured, dedicated, dignified, empowered, idealistic, intuitive, loyal, mature, regal, self sacrificing and tasteful.

Their negative traits are: domination, fanaticism, lack of taste, monopolization, pompousness, pettiness, snobbishness, superiority, treachery, uncivilized, and undignified.

Purple people can become very loyal and dedicated and will many times self-sacrifice themselves for their loved ones, careers, and projects. jesus paid the supreme self-sacrifice and now sits on a "Regal Throne". They will go to extreme details to finish any task they take on. The quotes, "that person has real class", and, "the pen is mightier then the sword", fit purple spiritual people more than any other color type. They would rather solve their differences with others in a civil and cultured manner, many times writing a formal letter expressing their displeasure and disagreement verses getting into a mundane vulgar physical battle with another person. They have an excellent ability to formulate words into a civilized, cultured, detailed and formal manner. This is why they dominate the career field of poetry, writing, editing and publishing. They are very conscience of their image and make excellent image consultants, "image is everything," is a quote that they truly understand. They love the arts and do very well as art dealers and cultural historians. Purple people also have excellent intuitive abilities, which make them natural psychics. The majority of the richest people in the world are purple spiritual people. I attribute this to their main character traits of power and dedication. They become very dedicated down to the details of their career jobs, and have created the majority of the most powerful businesses in the world.

Your favorite spiritual center colors will look and feel very cheerful, clean, creative, happy, imaginative, moral, spacious, spirited and wholesome on and around you. Use your spiritual center colors to create these images and feelings in your wardrobe and home-decor. The purple spectrum ranges from light lavenders, true hue purple and deep violets. Go to the color fans in the photo section of the book and determine your favorite purple spiritual center colors, then go to the 3-part chart in the back of the book and record them.

NATURAL CAREER FIELDS THAT PURPLE SPIRITUAL PEOPLE EXCEL IN:

Art Dealers, Creating Powerful Business empires, Cultural Historians, Editors, Image Consultants, Photographers, Poets, Psychics, Publishers and Writers.

Writers

Adrian (W)aller	(B)arbara Michaels	(B)etty Ren (W)right
Aimee (B)ender	(B)arbara (P)ark	(B)everly (B)arton
Alan (P)aton	(B)arbara Taylor (B)radford	(B)iasco (I)banez
Alan (W)atts	(B)arbara (W)alker	(B)ill (B)lum
Alec (W)augh	(B)arbara (W)inter	(B)ill (B)radley
Alexander (P)ope	(B)arbara (W)rede	(B)ill (B)ryson
Alfred North (W)hitehead	(B)arri (B)ryan	(B)ill Cosby
Alice (W)alker	(B)arry Sears	(B)ill Lauren
Ambrose (B)ierce	(B)arry Stoam	(B)ill McDonagill
Amy (B)auman	(B)eatrice (P)otter	(B)ill O' Rielly
Amy (B)owllan	(B)en (B)ova	(B)illie Letts
Anne (P)erry	(B)en Franklin	(B)illy Collins
Anne Hall (W)hitt	(B)ernard (B) Kerik	(B)illy (W)ilder
Anne Marie (W)inston	(B)ernard Cook	(B)ob (B)erkowitz
Annette (B)roadrick	(B)ernard Cooper	(B)ob (W)eil
Annie (P)roulx	(B)ernard Cornwell	(B)ob (W)oodward
Anthony (B)urgess	(B)ernard Goldberg	(B)ob Arnot
Anthony (P)owell	(B)ernard Lewis	(B)ob (B)igelow
Arna (B)ontemps	(B)ernhard Schlink	(B)ob Dole
Arnold (B)ennett	(B)ernice Spitzer	(B)ob Greene
Art (B)eroff	(B)ertrand Russell	(B)ob Morris
(B)arbara (B)oswell	(B)ertrice Small	(B)ob Rosner
(B)arbara Cartland	(B)eth Anderson	(B)obbie Ann Ross
(B)arbara Daly	(B)eth Gutcheon	(B)onita Quesinberry
(B)arbara DeAngelis	(B)eth Henderson	(B)onnie Drury
(B)arbara Delinsky	(B)etsy (B)yars	(B)oris (P)astemak
(B)arbara Hambly	(B)ette Edie	(B)rad Aronson
(B)arbara Kingsolver	(B)etty (B)eale	(B)rad (B)lanton
(B)arbara McMahon	(B)etty Neels	(B)radley Gerstman

(B)rad Meltzer
(B)rad Thor
(B)reena Clark
(B)renda Joyce
(B)rendan Francis
(B)renda Novak
(B)rett Lott
(B)ret Harte
(B)rian J. Karem
(B)rian Shapiro
(B)rian (W.) Aldiss
(B)rian (W)eiss
(B)rian (W)ildsmith
(B)ruce H. (W)ilkinson
(B)ruce Hart
(B)stan-D'zin-Rgy
(B)url (B)arer
C.N. (B)ean
C.N. (W)are
Caroline (P)reston
Catherine (G)eorge
Catherine (W)hitney
Cesare (P)avese
Charles (B)audelaire
Charles (B)erlitz
Charles (B)racket
Charlotte (B)yett-Compo
Cherie (B)ennett
Chris (B)achelder
Chris (B)aron
Chris (B)ohjalian
Christopher (P)aul Curtis
Christopher (P)izzo
Cindy (P)enn
Connie (B)riscoe
Connie (B)rockway
Cynthia (P)owell
Dale (B)rown
Daniel (P)etrocelli
Dave (B)arry
Dave (B)erry
Dave (P)elzer
David (B)aldalli
David (B)owman
Debra (W)ebb
Deborah (W)illis Ryan
Dewayne (W)ickhem

Dannion (B)rinkley
Darlene (B)ishop
Diane (P)almer
Diana (W)hitney
Dixie (B)rowning
Dorothy (P)arker
Dorothy (W)est
Dr. (B)enjamin Spock
Dr. Denis (W)aitley
Dr. (I)ra (P)rogoff
Dr. (P)eter (W)ashington
Dr. (W)alter (B)ortz
Dr. Nathaniel (B)randon
E.(B.) (W)hite
E.C. (P)ielou
Earl (W)oods
Edgar (W)allace
Edgar Allen (P)oe
Edgar Rice (B)urroughs
Edith (W)harton
Edith Jones Newbold
(W)harton
Edmund (W)hite
Edward (B)ellamy
Edward De (B)ono
E(i)leen (W)ilks - E is silent
Elie (W)iesel
Ellen (B)en Sefer
Elizabeth (B)arrett (B)rowning
Elizabeth (B)erg
Elizabeth (B)everly
Elizabeth (B)owen
Ellis (P)arker (B)utler
Emily (B)ronte
Erma (B)rombeck
Ernest (B)ramah
Ernest (P)apa Hemmingway
Esther (P)opel
Eudora (W)elty
Evan (I)nnes
Eve (B)abitz
Evelyn (W)augh
Faye (W)attelton
Fay (W)eldon
Felicia (W)illett
Francine (P)ascal
Francis (P)algrar

Fred (I)mus
Freeman (W)illis
Gail (B)radney
Gary (P)aulsen
Gayle (B)uck
Gayle (W)ilson
G.C. (W)aro
George (B)ernard Shaw
George (P)limpton
George (W)est
Gerald A. (B)rowne
Gina (W)ilkins
Ginny (W)illiams
Giuliano (B)ugiallis
Gretchen (B)rinck
Gwen (B)ristow
Gwendolyn (B.)(B)ennett
Gwendolyn (B)rooks
H.G. (W)ells
Harold (B)loom
Harriet (B)eecher Stowe
Harry (B)rown
Helen (B)ranchin
Henry (W)adsworth
Longfellow
Herman (W)ouk
Hilaire (B)elloc
Honore De (B)alzac
(I)an Fleming
(I)an McEwan
(I)da (B.)(W)ells-(B)arnett
(I)mamu A. (B)araka
(I)ra (B)erkow
(I)ra (B)erlin
(I)ra Gershwin
(I)rene Allen
(I)rene Hannon
(I)rene)(P)ence
(I)ris Murdoch
Irving (B)abbit
(I)saac (B)aber
(I)saac (B)ashevis Singer
(I)saac Newton
(I)sabelle Allende
(I)sak Dinesen
(I)srael Zangwill
(I)ssac Asimov

(I)van Klima
(I)van Turgenef
(I)vor Horton
(I)yanla Vanejart
Jack (B)roughton
Jack (P)relutsky
Jack (W)elch
James A.(B)aldwin
James (B)urke
James Van (P)raagh
James (W)eldon Johnson
James (W)itcomb Riley
Jan (B)rett
Janine (W)edel
J.(B.)(P)riestley
Jeanne (W)illiams
Jeannie Marie (B)oydon
Jeff (P). (P)aoiwa
Jennifer (B)aker
Jerry (P)ournelle
Jessamyn (W)est
Jimmy (B)reslin
Jo (B)everly
Joan (B)ears
Joan (B)ramsch
Joan S. (P)opek
Joan (W)ebster Anderson
Joan (W)olf
Joan Elliot (P)ickart
Joan Greenleaf (W)hittier
John (B)erry (B)arlow
John (B)arth
John (B)radshaw
John (B)runner
John (B)unyon
John (B)urdick
John (B)urnham Schwartz
John (P)ezan
John Dos (P)assos
John Greenleaf (W)hittier
John Stanley (W)eyman
Jorge Luis (B)orges
Joseph (B)rodsky
Joseph (P)ulitzer
Joseph (W)ambaugh
Judith (B)owen
Judith (I)vory

Judith (W)illis
Judy (B)lume
Julia (B)yrne
Julie (B)eard
Karen (W)iesner
Kate (W)alker
Katherine A. (B)orges
Ken (B)lanchard
Kevin (P)owell
Mildred (W)irt (B)enson
Mylvin (B)ragg
Nikki (B)enjamin
Nina (B)angs
Nina (B)urleigh
Noah (W)ebster
Norman Vincent (P)eale
Octavia (B)utler
Octavio (P)az
Oliver (B)utterworth
Oprah (W)infrey
Orson (W)elles
Oscar (W)ilde
(P).D. James
(P)am Houston
(P)amela (B)auer
(P)amela (B)rowning
(P)amela (B)uford
(P)amela (W)hite
(P)amela Macaluso
(P)amela Morse
(P)amela Morsi
(P)amela Toth
(P)at (B)arker
(P)at Conroy
(P)at Frank
(P)atricia (B)ragg
(P)atricia Forsythe
(P)atricia Hagan
(P)atricia McLinn
(P)atricia (P)otter
(P)atricia Rasey
(P)atricia Ryan
(P)atricia Seybold
(P)atricia (W)addell
(P)atrick (P)ierce
(P)atsi (B)ale Cox
(P)atty Sleem

(P)aul Auster
(P)aul (B). Farrell
(P)aul (B)owes
(P)aul C.(B)ragg
(P)aul E. Erdman
(P)aul Gallic
(P)aul Hond
(P)aul Laurence Dunbar
(P)aul Meter
(P)aul Newman
(P)aul Robert (W)alker
(P)aul Saloman
(P)aul Vjecsner
(P)aula (P)arisi
(P)aula Marshall
(P)auline Maier
(P)earl Cleage
(P)earl S. (B)uck
(P)eggy (B)echko
(P)eggy Moreland
(P)eggy Tibbetts
(P)eggy (W)ibb
(P)enelope Fitzgerald
(P)enny Jordan
(P)enny Richards
(P)ercy (B)ysshe Shelley
(P)ersia Woolley
(P)ete (B)eard
(P)eter (B)iskind
(P)eter (B)ogdanovich
(P)eter (W)right
(P)eter Ackroyd
(P)eter Cappellli
(P)eter Greenberry
(P)eter Hamill
(P)eter Hamilton
(P)eter J. D'adamo
(P)eter James
(P)eter Straub
(P)J.(W)odehouse
(P)ierre Louys
(P)iers Anthony
Phillip (B)erman
Philip (P)ullman
Phyllis (W)elsh
Phyllis (W)heatley
Phyllis (W)hitney

(P)lutarch
(P)o (B)ronson
Rachael (W)ilson
Ralph (W)aldo Emerson
Randy (W)ayne (W)hite
Ray (B)radbury
Rebecca (B)randewyne
Rebecca (P)aisley
Rebecca (W)ells
Rebecca (W)est
Rebecca (W)inters
Renni (B)rowne
Reynolds (P)rice
Rhonda (B)ritten
Richard (B)ach
Richard (B)achwriter
Richard N. (B)olles
Richard North (P)atterson
Richard (P)rice
Richard (W)right
Rick (B)ass
Rita Mae (B)rown
Robert Anton (W)ilson
Robert (B)aer
Robert (B)arr
Robert (B)enchley
Robert (B)ly
Robert (B)ob (B)urns
Robert (B)rowning
Robert (B.) (P)arker
Robert (P)enn (W)arren
Robert (W)ise
Sam (P)eckinpau
Samuel (B)eckett
Samuel (B)utler
Saul (B)ellows
Saul (W)illiams
Sharon (P)atton
Sharon Tabor (W)arren
Shelley (B)radley
Sherryl (W)oods
Shri Haidakhan (B)abaji

Sir (W)alter Scott
S.K. (W)olf
Stephanie (B)ond
Steve (P)ieczenik
Stuart (W)oods
Susan (I)saacs
Suzzanne (B)rockmann
Tennessee (W)illiams
Terry L. (W)hite
Thomas (P)aine
Thomas (P)erry
Thorton (W)ilder
Tom (W)illard
Tom (W)olfe
Toni (B)lake
Toni Cade (B)ambara
Victoria (B)enson
Victoria (P)ade
Victoria (P)aige
Victor L. (W)hitechurch
Vincent (B)ugliosi
Virginia (W)oolf
(W). Somerset Maughn
(W). (B). Yeats
(W). E.B Griffin
(W). J. (W)eatherby
(W). R. Thompson
(W)ade Davis
(W)alker (P)ercy
(W)allace Stagner
(W)allace Stevens
(W)ally Lamb
(W)alter Lippmann
(W)alter Lord
(W)alter Mosezy
(W)alter Mosley
(W)alter (W)inchell
(W)alt (W)hitman
(W)arren (B)uffet
(W)ashington Irving
(W)ayne Dryer
(W)endy (B)eckett
(W)endy Loggia

(W)endy Shabit
(W)hitney Otto
(W)ilbur Libby
(W)ill Friedwald
(W)illa Cather
(W)illiam (B)ernhardth
(W)illiam (B)lake
(W)illiam Bradford Huie
(W)illiam (B)uckley
(W)illiam (B)urroughs
(W)illiam (B)utler Yeats
(W)illiam C. Triplett II
(W)illiam Danko
(W)illiam Faulkner
(W)illiam Gaines
(W)illiam Gibson
(W)illiam Golding
(W)illiam Kennedy
(W)illiam Kittridge
(W)illiam Le Queux
(W)illiam Lovejoy
(W)illiam Makepeace
Thackeray
(W)illiam (P)enn
(W)illiam Randolph Hearst
(W)illiam Shakespeare
(W)illiam Taylor Adams
(W)illiam Tynsdale
(W)illiam Vaughan Moody
(W)illiam (W)ordsworth
(W)inston Churchill
(W)illie Jolley
Yogi (B)erra

Purple Spectrum - Culture - Writing - Psychic
(B, I, P, W)

Purple spiritual center "dedicated" people who became the wealthiest and most powerful in their field of business.

Donald (B)ren
Edgar M (B)ronfman Sr.
Eli (B)road
H. Ross (P)erot
J. (P)aul Getty
Jeffery (P) (B)ezos
John (W)erner Kluge
Lillian (B)ettencourt

Micheal (B)loomberg
(P)ierre M Omidyar
(P)aul Allen
(P)rince Alwaleed (B)intal Alsaud
Robert A (P)ritzker
Ronald O (P)erelman
Steven A (B)allmer

Theodore (W) (W)aitt
Ty (W)arner
(W)alter M Annenberg
(W)alter Scott
(W)altons' of Walmart chain
(W)arren E (B)uffet
(W)illiam Gates
(W)illiam Hearst
(W)illiam R Hewlett

SAYINGS THAT STIMULATE PURPLE SPIRITUAL PEOPLE

Nations, like individuals, live or die, but civilization cannot perish. - Mazzini

Human beings . . . should become civilized, that is, so related to each other that their thinking is a concerted attempt to reach common answers to common problems. They should practice a friendliness of the mind. Violence . . . is savagery. Civilization is reasonableness. - Alexander Meiklejohn

A sufficient and sure method of civilization is the influence of good women. - Emerson

The old Hindu saw, in his dream, the human race led out to its various fortunes. First, men were in chains that went back to an iron hand. Then he saw them led by threads from the brain, which went upward to an unseen hand. The first was despotism, iron, and ruling by force. The last was civilization ruling by ideas. - Wendell Phillips

It is very rare to find ground, which produces nothing. If it is not covered with flowers, fruit trees, and grains, it is produces briars and pines. It is the same with man; if he is not virtuous, he becomes vicious.- Bruyere

It matters little whether a man be mathematically, or philologically, or artistically cultivated, so he be but cultivated. - Goethe

Cultivation to the mind is as necessary as food to the body. - Cicero

We never reach our ideals, whether of mental or moral improvement, but the thought of them shows us our deficiencies, and spurs us on to higher and better things. - Tryon Edwards

Every life has its actual blanks, which the ideal must fill up, or which else remain bare and profitless forever.- J.W. Howe

The best and noblest lives are those which are set toward high ideals. And the higher the noblest ideal that any man can have is Jesus of Nazareth. - Rene Almeras

RED SPIRITUAL PEOPLE

Red spiritual people are those who's first, middle only if used regularly, or last names start with red sounding letters of (C), (J), (Q), and (X). God's positive character attributes of the red spectrum are: beauty of manner (elegance), benevolence (sense of good will), charitableness, chivalry, compassion, courteous (mercifulness), gracefulness, gratefulness (thankfulness), honesty (sincerity), love, persistence (tenaciousness), physical life energy, romance and valor, (courage). (J)esus said if you do but one thing on this earth "Love one another."

The negative traits of the red spectrum are: brutality, dishonesty, excessive carnal desire, impulsiveness (impatience), jealousy (envy), physical egotism, physical laziness, pitilessness (lack of compassion), rudeness (coarseness), savageness (barbaric).

The red spectrum consists of the pink reds, rose reds, true hue red, cranberry reds and dark wine reds. Your favorite spiritual center colors will look and feel very cheerful, clean, creative, happy, imaginative, moral, spacious, spirited and wholesome on and around you. Use your spiritual center colors to create these images and feelings in your wardrobe and home-decor. Go to the color fans in the photo section of the book and determine your favorite red spiritual center colors, then go to the 3-part chart in the back of the book and record them.

NATURAL CAREER CHOICES THAT RED SPIRITUAL PEOPLE EXCEL IN:

Red spiritual people excel in the career fields of: athletics, charity organizers, jazz musicians, journalists, medical, physical exercise gurus, health food authors and advocates, romantic writers, romantic talk show hosts, and truth talk show hosts.

Famous Red Spiritual Center Doctors, Health Authors and Physical Fitness Enthusiasts
Some G's sound to J

(C)harles Atlas	(J)ake - Bodies by Jake
(C)harles Roman	(J)ane Brody
(C). W. Post	(J)ane Fonda
Debbie (S)iebers - (S) sounds to C	(J)ay Cordich
Dr. Bernard (S)iegel- (S) sounds to C	(J)ean Carper
Dr. (C) Evert Coop	(J)enny Craig
Dr. (C)harles R. Drew	(J)erome Irving Rodale
Dr. (J)oel D. Wallach	(J)ethro Kloss
Dr. (J)ohn Birch	(J)im Karas
Dr. (J)ohn La Puma	(J)im Ward
Dr. Percy Lavon (J)ulian	(J)oanie Greggins
President (G)eorge W. Bush	(J)oe Wielder
(G)eorge Washington Carver	(J)ohn Basedow
Gil (J)anklowic	(J)ohn Harvey Post
(J)ackie (C)han	(J)oy Bauer
(J)ack La Lanne	(J)yl Stienback
(J)ack Palance --doing push ups on Academy Awards Show and in front of congressman.	

Red Spectrum - Romance - Physical Life Forces - Graceful - Truthfulness
(C, J, Q, X)

Red Spiritual Center
Romantic Writers and Romantic Relationship Authors

(C)herry Adair
(J)ack Prelutsky
(J)ackie Merritt
(J)acqueline Diamond
(J)ane Aiken Hodge
(J)ane Anderson
(J)ane Ann Krentz
(J)ane Feathers
(J)ane Futcher
(J)ane McFann
(J)ane Peart
(J)anelle Denison
(J)anet Dailey
(J)anet Oke
(J)an McDaniel
(J)ayne Ann Krentz
(J)ayne Castle
(J)ean Brasher
(J)eanne Lancour

(J)enelle Denison
(J)ennifer Archer
(J)ennifer Baker
(J)ennifer Cruise
(J)essamyn West
(J)essica Hart
(J)essie Kennedy
(J)oan Hessayon
(J)oan Lowery Nixon
(J)oanne Rock
(J)o Ann Ferguson
(J)oan Wolf
(J)o Beverley
(J)odi O'Donnell
(J)oe Cottonwood
(J)ohanna Lindsey
(J)ohn Burdick
(J)ohn Gray

(J)o Leigh
(J)oshua Harris
(J)oyce Ames
(J)udith Bowen
(J)udith Ivory
(J)udith Landsdowne
(J)udith O'Brien
(J)udy Christenberg
(J)ulie Beard
(J)ulie Kenner
(J)ulie McBride
(J)ulie Tetel Andresen
Brenda (J)oyce
Kathryn (J)ensen
Mary (J)o Putney
Muriel (J)ensen
Penny (J)ordan
Tara Taylor (Q)uinn

Red Spiritual Center
Talk Show Hosts:

(C)harlie Rose
(C)hevy (C)hase
(J)ack Parr
(J)ane Parr
(J)ane Whitney
(J)ay Leno
(J)enny (J)ones
(J)erry Springer
(J)oan Rivers
(J)oe Fish
(J)oey Bishop
(J)ohnny Carson
Dr. (J)oy Browne
Morton Downey (J)r.
Sally (J)esse Raphael

Red Spiritual Center
Romantic Show Hosts:

(C)huck Woolery
(J)im Lang

Red Spiritual Center
Journalists:

(C)harles Krauthammer
(C)harles Kuralt
(C)harles Osgood
(C)het Huntley
Connie (C)hung
(G)eorge F. Will
(J)ane Pauley
(J)ean Stalling
(J)immy Breslin
(J)ohn (C)hancellor
(J)ohn (C) Dvorak
(J)ohn Hollman
(J)udy Woodruff
Peter (J)ennings
P.(J.)O'Rourke
Sydney (J.) Harris
William F Buckley (J)r.
William Randolph Hearst (J)r.

Red Spiritual Center
Jazz Musicians:

Ahamd (J)amal
Blind Lemon (J)efferson
Cal T(j)ader - T is silent
(C)edar Walton
(C)harlie Byrd
(C)harlie Haden
(C)harlie Parker
(C)harles Mingus
(C)hick Webb
(C)hic Correa
(C)hubby (J)ackson
Etta (J)ones
Gary (J)ohns
Glover Washington (J)r.
(G)eorge Gerswin
(G)eorge V. (J)ohnson
(G)eorge Mitchell -
(G) sounds to J
Hank (J)ones
Harry (J)ames
Herb (J)effries
(J)acki Cooper
(J)ack Teagardern
(J)ames P. (J)ohnson
(J)anis (S)iegal -
(S) sounds to c

(J)ean Goldkette
(J)elly Roll Morton
(J)eri Southern
(J)ess Stacy
(J)immy McPartland
(J)immy Noone
(J)immy Rushing
(J)oe King Oliver
(J)oe Venuti
(J)ohn Coltrane
(J)ohn Lindsay
(J)ohnny Dodds
(J)ohnny Griffin
(J)ohnny St. Cyr
(J)osephine Baker
(J)o Stafford
(J)oya Sherrill
(J)ulian Cannonball Adderley
(J)ulie London
(J)une Christy
Kennedy (J)enson
Scott (J)oplin
Shelly (J)ordon
(Q)uincy (J)ones
(X)avier Cougart

Love gives itself; it is not bought. - Longfellow

Love, which is only an episode in the life of man, is the entire history of woman's life.
-Mad. de Stael

The motto of chivalry is also the motto of wisdom: to serve all, but love only one. - Balzac

The treasures of the deep are not so precious as are the concealed comforts of a man locked up in woman's love. - Middleton

Affections, like the conscience, are rather to be led than drawn: and 'tis to be feared, they that marry where they do not love, will love where they do not marry. - Fuller

We are shaped and fashioned by what we love. - Goethe

When the mind loses its feeling for elegance, it grows corrupt and groveling, and seeks in the crowd what ought to be found at home. - Landor

The heart of him who truly loves is a paradise on earth: he has God in himself,
for God is love. -Lamennais

I am not one of those who do not believe in love at first sight, but I believe in taking a second look. - Lamennais

I have enjoyed the happiness of the world: I have lived and loved. - Schiller

Let grace and goodness be the principal loadstone of thy affections. For love which hath ends, will have an end: whereas that which is founded on true virtue, will always continue. - Dryden

Passion may be blind: but to say that love is, is a libel and a lie. - Nothing is more sharp-sighted or sensitive than true love, in discerning, as by an instinct, the feeling of another. - W.H. Davis

Love is an image of God, and not a lifeless image, but the living essence of the divine nature, which beams full of all goodness. - Luther

Absence in love is like water upon fire: a little quickens, but much extinguishes it. - Hannah More

It is better to have loved and lost, than not to love at all. - Tennyson

The plainest man that can convince a woman that he is really in love with her, has done more to make her in love with him than the handsomest man, if he can produce no such conviction. For the love of woman is a shoot, not a seed, and flourishes most vigorously only when engrafted on that love which is rooted in the breast of another. - Colton

ORANGE SPIRITUAL PEOPLE

Orange spiritual people are those who's first, middle only if used regularly, or last names start with a (D), (K), (R), or (Y) sounding letters. God's positive character traits of orange spiritual people are: affection (fondness), caring, creativity, inspirational enthusiasm, joyfulness, kindness (warm heartedness), repentance, self-assurance, speculation, venturesome and versatile.

The negative traits are: boastfulness, despair (depression), destructiveness, exhibitionism, flamboyance and unpleasantness. Your favorite spiritual center colors will look and feel very cheerful, clean, creative, happy, imaginative, moral, spacious, spirited, and wholesome, on and around you. Use your spiritual center colors to create these images and feelings in your wardrobe and home-decor. The orange spectrum ranges from the light peaches, light corals, true hue orange, rust, and dark earthy rust oranges. Go to the color fans in the photo section of the book and determine your favorite orange spiritual center colors, then go to the 3-part chart in the back of the book and record them.

Orange spiritual people are the most affectionate, caring, creative, kindest, and warmest, of all the color types. When operating off of the positive character traits of the orange spectrum, they excel in career fields that require these qualities. Orange people, depending on which centers their orange letters in their names are attuned to, dominate many career fields, as you will learn by reading the other orange center sections of this book. This I attribute to the "creative" character attribute of this spectrum.

NATURAL CAREER CHOICES THAT ORANGE SPIRITUAL PEOPLE EXCEL IN:

Orange Spectrum - Creativity - Kindness - Versatility
(D, K, R, Y)*   *C's may sound to K   *ia may sound to Y   *tt may sound to D
Orange Spiritual Center Creative Artists:

Aaron (D)ouglas
Alander (C)abanel
Albercht (D)urer
Alexander (C)alder
Alexander Francois (D)esportes
Allan (R)amsy
Alonso (C)ano
Andrea (D)el Verrocchio
Andre (D)erain
Andrey (R)yabushkin
Angelica (K)auffman
Anselm (K)iefer
Antoine (C)aron
Anton (R)aphael Mengs
Arkhip (K)uinji
Arthur (D)ove
Auguste (D). Ingres

Auguste (R)odin
Bathasar Van (D)er Ast
Besto (K)azaishvilli
Blaine (K)ern
Bob (R)oss
Bondone (D)i Giotto
Bridget (R)iley
Buoninssegna (D)i (D)uccio
(C)amille Pissaro
(C)anacci
(C)analetto
(C)aravaggio
(C)arel Fabritius
(C)arl Ludwig Joham
(C)hristineck
(C)arracci
(C)aspar (D)avid Friedrich
Charles (D)e La Fosse

(C)hristo
(C)laes Oldenburg
(C)laude Lorrain
(C)laude Monet
(C)lementine
(C)lorret
(C)onstantin (K)orovin
(C)ornelis (D)e Vos
(C)orreggio
(C)osme Tura
(C)ount Fedor Tolstoy
(D)aniel Seghers
(D)ante Gabriel (R)ossetti
(D)avid Alfaro Sequeiros
D)avid (C)owles
(D)avid Hockney
(D)avid Smith
(D)ebra Butterfield

(D)iane Arbus
(D)iego (R)ivera
(D)iego Velazquez
(D)ieric Bouts
(D)irck Hals
(D)irk Van Baburen
(D)mitry Levizky
(D)ominico Ghircandaio
(D)onna (D)ewsberry
(D)orothea Lange
(D)orothea Tanning
(D)osso (D)ossi
Edgar (D)agas
Elaine (D)e (K)ooning
Elizabeth (C)atlett
Ellsworth (K)elly
Eugene (D)elacroix
Evgraf (K)rendovsky
Faith (R)ingbold
Fedor (R)obotov
Francesco (D)el (C)ossa
Francisco (D)e Goya
Francisco (D)e Zurbaran
Frank (K)line
Frederick (R)emington
Frida (K)ahlo
George (C)atlin
Georges (D)e La Tour
Georges (R)ouault
Georgia O' (K)eefe
Georgio (D)e Chirico
Gerald (D)avid
Giovanni Battista Cima (D)a
(C)onegliano
Gustave (C)allibotte
Gustave (D)ore
Gustave (K)limt
Henri (C)arier Bresson
Henri (D)e Toulouse-Lautrec
Henri Met (D)e Bles
Henri (R)ousseau
Honre (D)aumier
Hugo Van (D)er Goes
Ilya (R)ipin
Ivan (K)hrutsky
Ivan (K)ramskoy
Irene (R)ice Pereira
Jacques Louis (D)avid

Jan (D)avid (D)e Heem
Jasper (C)ropsey
Jean Auguste (D)ominique
Ingres
Jean Baptiste (C)amille
(C)orot
Jean (D)ubuffet
Jean Francois (D)e Troy
Jennifer (D)urrant
Jim (D)ine
John (R)hoden
John (R)uskins
Jorge (R)ubell
Joelynn (D)uesberry
John (C)ontestable
John Singleton (C)opley
Joseph (C)ornell
Jusepe (D)e (R)ibera
(K)ano Tanya
(K)apiton Zelenstov
(K)arl Brullof
(K)ashmir Malevich
(K)atsushika Hokusai
(K)eith Haring
(K)elly (K)ollwitz
(K)onrad Witz
Larry (R)ivers
Laurent (D)e La Hue
Leonardo (d)a Vinci
Le(r)oy Neiman
Lewis (C)arol
Lucas (C)ranach
Man (R)ay
Marcell (D)uchamp
Mark (R)othko
Mary (C)assatt
Maurice (d)e Valminck
Mildred (D)idrikson
Nicholas (D)e Largilliere
Nikifor (K)rylov
Norman (R)ockwell
Odilon (R)edon
Orest (K)iprensky
Paul (K)lee
Peter Paul (R)ubens
Petrus (C)hristus
Piero (D)i (C)osimo
Pierre Auguste (R)enoir

Pierre Puvis (D)e Chavannes
Pieter (D)e Hooch
Pietro (C)avallini
Philips (K)oninck
(R)aymond Hu
(R)ed Grooms
(R)emedios Varo
(R)ichard (D)iebenkorn
(R)ichard Barthe
(R)ichard Bresnahan
(R)ichard Hunt
(R)ichard Serra
(R)idolfo Ghirlandaio
(R)obert (C)ampin
(R)obert (D)uncanson
(R)obert Feke
(R)obert Indiana
(R)obert (R)auschenbers
(R)obert Motherwell
(R)ojier Van (d)er Weyden
(R)omare Bearden
(R)on B. (K)itaj
(R)osa Bonheur
(R)osalba (C)arriera
(R)oy Lichenstein
Salvador (D)ali
Sanzio (R)aphael
Shimomura (K)anzan
Sir Anthony Van (D)yck
Sir (D)avid Wilkie
Sir Edward (C)oley Burne
Jones
Sir Henry (R)ueburn
Sonia (D)elaunay
Stuart (D)avis
Tamara (D)e Lempicka
Teresa (D)el Pol
Theodore (R)ousseau
Thomas (C)ole
Thomas (C)outure
Thomas (K)incaid
Van (R)ijn (R)embrandt
Vinnie (R)eam Hoxie
Walt (D)isney
Wassily (K)andinsky
Willem (D)e (K)ooning
(Y)asui Sutaro

Orange Spectrum - Creativity - Kindness - Versatility
(D, K, R, Y)*   *C's may sound to K   *ia may sound to Y   *tt may sound to D
Orange Physical Center
Designers:

Anne (K)lein
Bonnie (C)ashin
(C)alvin Klein
(C)arolina Herrera
(C)hristian (D)ior
(C)hristian Lacroix
(C)hristina Perrin
(C)laire McCardell
(C)lements (R)iberio
(C)omme (D)es Garcons
(C)ourreges
Cynthia (R)owley
(D)anenberg (C)astro
(D)aniel Herman
(D)aniela Vettori
(D)aryl (K)errigans

(D)iane Von Furstenberg
(D)ior
(D)onna (K)aran
(D)onatella Versace
(D)ries Van Noten
Emma (C)ook
Gabriel (C)oco Chanel
Gilles (D)ufour
Helen (R)ose
John (R)ocha
(K)arl Lagerfeld
(K)enneth (C)ole
(K)enzo
Le(r)oy Neiman
Lilly (D)asha
Maggy (R)ouff
Michael (K)ors

Narcisco (R)odrique
Nina (R)icci
Olge (C)assini
Orie (K)elly
Oscar (D)e La (R)enta
Pamela (D)ennis
Pierre (C)ardin
(R)alph Lauren
(R)alph (R)icci
(R)andolph (D)uke
(R)ichard Tyler
(R)oberto (C)avalli
(R)oy Halston Frowick
(R)udy Gernreich
Sonia (R)ykiel
William (C)ahill

Orange Spectrum - Creativity - Kindness - Versatility
(D, K, R, Y)*
*C's may sound to K
Orange Spiritual Center
Authors or Experts in - Advertising - Marketing - Promotional Fields

Burt (D)ubin
Charles (K)essler
(C)olonel Tom Parker
(C)orey (R)udl
(C)raig (C)ampana
(D)ale (C)arnegie
(D)ale Irwin
(D)ana Burke
(D)an (C)ooper
(D)aniel Harrison
(D)an (K)ennedy
(D)an Poynter
(D)an Seidman
(D)avid Garfinkle

(D)avid Ogilvy
(D)ebbie Allen
(D)ebbie Bermont
(D)eb Haggerty
(D)on (K)ing
(D)on Taylor
(D)oug Smart
Howard (C)osell
Jay (C)onrad Levinson
Jean (D)esmond
Jeff (R)ubin
Jim (C)athcart
John (K)remer
(K)aren Lawson
(K)en Blanchard

Marilyn (R)oss
Melanie (R)oetken
(R)aleigh Pinskey
(R)enee Walkup
(R)ick Segal
(R)obert (D)avis
(R)ochelle Balch
(R)on Arden
(R)on Popeil
(R)oseann Higgins
Silvana (C)lark
Susan (R)oAne
T.J.(R)eid
(Y)anik Silver

SAYINGS THAT STIMULATE ORANGE SPIRITUAL PEOPLE

A person who does not construct in work or kindness, destructs, or does nothing at all. Take your pick between the three. - D.G. Rolliet

The drying up a single tear has more of honest fame, than the shedding seas of gore. - Byron

To cultivate kindness is a valuable part of the business of life. - Johnson

Make a rule, and pray to God to help you to keep it, never, if possible, to lie down at night without being able to say: "I have made on human being at least a little wiser, or a little happier, or at least a little better this day". - Charles Kingsley

A word of kindness is seldom spoken in vain, while witty sayings are as easily lost as the pearls slipping from a broken string - G.D. Prentice

Kindness in women, not their beauteous looks shall win my love. - Shakespeare

Sow good services; sweet remembrances will grow from them. - Madame de Stael

Jesus and Socrates, out of very different backgrounds, are saying the same thing. Intelligence is kindness. Kindness is intelligence. The fundamental, which the two terms suggest in different ways . . . is the same quality on which all human civilization is built. - Alexander Meiklejohn

I expect to pass through life but once. If therefore, there be any kindness I can show, or any good thing I can do to any fellow-being, let me do it now, and not defer or neglect it, as I shall not pass this way again. -Penn

I have sped much by land, and sea, and mingled with many people, but never yet could find a spot unsunned by human kindness. - Tupper

Kindness is the golden chain by which society is bound together. - Goethe

Kindness is a language the dumb can speak, and the deaf can hear and understand. - Bovee

When death, the great reconciler, has come, it is never our tenderness that we repent of, but our severity. - George Eliot

What do we live for, if it is not to make life less difficult to each other? - George Eliot

The true and noble way to kill a foe, is not to kill him; you, with kindness, may so change him that he shall cease to be a foe, and then he's slain. - Aleyn

Ask thyself, daily, to how many ill-minded persons thou hast shown a kind disposition.- Marcus Antoninus

He that will not give some portion of his ease, his blood, his wealth, for others' good, is a poor, frozen churl. - Joanna Baillie

Both man and womankind - belie their nature when they are not kind. - G. Bailey

Kind words produce their own image in men's souls; and a beautiful image it is. They soothe and quiet and comfort the hearer. They shame him out of his sour, morose, unkind feelings. We have not yet begun to use kind words in such abundance, as they ought to be used. - Pascal

Kindness in ourselves is the honey that blunts the sting of unkindness in another. - Landor

YELLOW SPIRITUAL PEOPLE

Yellow spiritual people are those whose first, middle only if used routinely, or last names start with (E), (L), (S) or (Z) sounding letters. Yellow is God's intellectual and analytical color. It is also the positive thinking, cheerful, and optimistic spectrum. God's other positive character attributes of this spectrum are: clarity, comprehension, decisiveness, glorification (of God), logic, and reasonableness. Yellow truly is the mental color. Yellow people are very quick thinkers and they usually learn quickly and are big believers of positive thinking philosophies and tend to dominate this field as you will see in the following list of yellow career choices. Yellow people excel in analytical, educational and scientific fields, or where there is a need for cheerfulness, friendliness, logic, and mental grasp. Yellow people stress the need for education in the lives of others and often continue to try to acquire new knowledge throughout their entire life.

Here are the negative character traits that yellow spiritual people must guard against: conniving, deception, pessimism, shrewdness and vindictiveness. The yellow spectrum consists of the light pale yellow's, true hue yellow, gold yellow's and dark copper yellow's. Your favorite spiritual center colors will look and feel very cheerful, clean, creative, happy, imaginative, moral, spacious, spirited and wholesome, on and around you. Use your spiritual center colors to create these images and feelings in your wardrobe and home-decor. Go to the color fans in the photo section of the book and determine your favorite yellow spiritual center colors, then go to the 3-part chart in the back of the book and record them.

NATURAL CAREER CHOICES THAT YELLOW SPIRITUAL PEOPLE EXCEL IN:

(E, L, S, Z) Famous Yellow Spiritual Center Educators and Contributors to Education Institutions:

Anne (S)ullivan
(E)leanor Roosevelt
(E)lihu Yale
(J)acques Costeau - J sounds to Z
(L)ee (S)trasberg
(L)eland (S)tanford
(L)eonardo da Vinci
(L)eo Rosten
Norma (L)orre Goodrich
(S)ally (L) (S)mith
(S)ara Bernhardt
(S)ocrates
Wendy (E)wald

Yellow Spiritual Center Positive Thinking Philosophers:

(L)eo Bascquila
(L). Ron Hubbard
(L)es Brown
(L)ouise Hay
(S)haki Gawain

Famous Yellow Spiritual Center Cheerful Celebrities:

Art (L)inkletter
David (L)etterman
(E)ddie Murphy
(E)lton John
Jack (L)emon
Jay (L)eno
Jerry (L)ewis
(L)awernce Welk
(L)eslie Nielson
(L)iberace
(L)iza Minelli
(L)ou Costello
(L)ouis Armstrong
(L)uciano Pavarotti
(L)ucielle Ball
(L)ucy (L)iu
Mario (L)anza
(S)ally Fields
(S)ammy Davis Jr.
(S)andy Duncan
(S)heri (L)ewis
(S)hirley Maclaine
(S)hirley Temple-Black
(S)teve Allen
(S)teve Irwin
Red (S)kelton
Richard (S)immons

Famous Yellow Spiritual Center Sales People:

(E)stee (L)auder
(S)am Walton
(S)teven Jobs

Yellow Mental Center Intellects

A(l)bert Einstein
A(l)exander Graham B(e)ll
A(l)exander Hamilton
A(l)fred Nobel
C(l)are Booth
Daniel W(e)bster
E(l)i Whitney
H(e)len Hayes
H(e)len K(e)ller
H(e)nry Ford
H(e)nry Hudson
H(e)nry Stanley
I(s)aac N(e)wton
J(e)rome L(e)melson
L(e)onardo Da Vinci
L(e)e D(e) Foster
Noah W(e)bster
P(i)erre Currie- (i) sounds to e
P(l)ato
P(l)iny
Sara B(e)rnhardt
Thomas J(e)fferson

SAYINGS THAT STIMULATE YELLOW SPIRITUAL PEOPLE:

What sunshine is to flowers, smiles are to humanity. They are but trifles, to be sure; but, scattered along life's pathway, the good they do is inconceivable.

Be cheerful; do not brood over fond hopes unrealized until a chain is fastened on each thought and wound around the heart. Nature intended you to be the fountain-spring of cheerfulness and social life. Not the monument of despair and melancholy. - A. Helps

Logic and metaphysics make use of more tools than all the rest of the sciences put together, and they do the least work. - Colton

A cheerful temper joined with innocence will make beauty attractive, knowledge delightful, and wit good natured. It will lighten sickness, poverty, and affliction; convert ignorance into an amiable simplicity, and render deformity itself agreeable. - Addison

If I can put one touch of a rosy sunset into the life of any man or woman, I shall feel that I have worked with God. - G. MacDonald

Cheerfulness is health; its opposite, melancholy, is disease. - Halibuton

Wondrous is the strength of cheerfulness, and its power of endurance - the cheerful man will do more in the same time, will do it better, will persevere in it longer, than the sad or sullen. - Carlyle

Get into the habit of looking for the silver lining of the cloud, and when you have found it, continue to look at it, rather than at the leaden gray in the middle. It will help you over many hard places. - Willitts

If good people would but make their goodness agreeable, and smile instead of frowning in their virtue, how many would they win to the good cause. - Usher

It was a saying of the ancients, that "truth lies in a well;" and to carry on the metaphor, we may justly say, that logic supplies us with steps whereby we may go down to reach the water. - Watts

Cheerfulness is as natural to the heart of a man in strong health , as color to his cheek; and wherever there is habitual gloom, there must be either bad air, unwholesome food, improperly severe labor, or erring habits of life. - Ruskin

God is glorified, not by our groans but by our thanksgivings; and all good thought and good action claim a natural alliance with good cheer. - E.P. Whipple

Be cheerful always, There is no path but will be easier traveled, no load but will be lighter, no shadow on heart and brain but will lift sooner for a person of determined cheerfulness.

Logic is the art of convincing us of some truth. - Bruyere

Oh, give us the man who sings at his work. - Carlyle

The highest wisdom is continual cheerfulness; such a state, like the region above the moon, is always clear and serene. - Montaigne

You have not fulfilled every duty unless you have fulfilled that of being cheerful
and pleasant. - C. Buxton

GREEN SPIRITUAL PEOPLE

Green spiritual people are those whose first, middle only if used regularly, or last names start with (F), (M), or (T), sounding letters. Green is God's spectrum of balance, control (self-control), and peacefulness. God's other positive traits of the green spectrum are: caution, cooperation, critical, discrimination, equitableness (agreeableness), impartiality (fairness), lawfulness, and poise.

The negative traits are: bias, callousness, disagreeableness, envy, lack of judgment, miserliness, sense of injustice and suspicion. I also call green the ego color; green spiritual people must operate off a spiritual level verses an ego level and must be careful not to get into ego battles with others. If a green spiritual person is truly poised, in-control and peaceful, they will not let their ego get involved in a one-upmanship battle with another. Green spiritual people must also guard against playing the macho, ego, role. Your favorite spiritual center colors will look and feel very cheerful, clean, creative, happy, imaginative, moral, spacious, spirited and wholesome on and around you. Use your spiritual center colors to create these images and feelings in your wardrobe and home-decor. Go to the color fans in the photo section of the book and determine your favorite green spiritual center colors, then go to the 3-part chart in the back of the book and record them. The green spectrum ranges from light mint green, true hue green to dark forest green.

NATURAL CAREER CHOICES THAT GREEN SPIRITUAL PEOPLE EXCEL IN:

Green Spectrum - Poise - Balance - Justice - Peacefulness
(F, M, T)
Green Spiritual Center Architects:

Arthur B. (M)ullet
Bernard (M)aybeck
Carlo (M)aderno
Charles (F)ollen (M)cKim
Charles Rennie (M)ackintosh
Edla (M)uir
Elizabeth (M)artini
(F)ilippo Brunelleschi
(F)lorence Cuscomb
(F)rancesco Borromini
(F)rancois De Cuvillies
(F)rank (F)urness
(F)rank Gehry
(F)rank Lloyd Wright
(F)redrick Olemstead
(F)rei Otto
John (F)rancis
John (M)iller
Julia (M)organ
Louis Christian (M)ullgradt
Lutah (M)aria Riggs

Ludwig (M)usvander Rohe
(M)arcia (M)ead
(M)argarete Schautte Lihotzky
(M)argaret Hicks
(M)arie (F)rommer
(M)arion (M)ahony Griffin
(M)ary Hommann
(M)ary Otis Stevens
(M)aya Ling Lin
(M)ichelangelo Buonarroti
(M)ichelozzi (M)ichelozzo
(M)ike Graves
(M)inevra Parker
(M)inow Yamasaki
(M)iny Pei
(M)nesikles
(M)oshe Safdie
Norman (F)oster
(P)hillip Johnson

(P)hillip Speakman Webb -
p sounds to f
(P)hyllis Lambert - p sounds to f
Pierre (F)ontaine
Richard Buckminister (F)uller
Richard (M)eier
Robert (M)ills
Samuel (M)cIntire
Sophie (T)aeuber
(T)ange Venzo
(T)erry (F)irnando Belaunde
(T)heodate Pope Riddle
(T)hierry Despont
(T)homas Hamilton
(T)homas Jefferson
(T)homas Sully
(T)homas Ustick Walter
(T)homas Walter
(T)ony Smith
(T).Y. Lin
William (T)horton

49

Green Spiritual & Physical Center
Quarterbacks:

Alex Van Pel(t)
An(t)hony Wrigh(t)
Bar(t) Starr
Ber(t) Jones
Billy Joe (T)olliver
Bob Wa(t)er(f)ield
Boo(m)er Easiason
Bren(t) (T)il(f)er
Bre(tt) (F)arve
Bubby Bris(t)er
Cade (M)cNown
Chad Penning(t)on
Chris Red(m)an
Cli(ff) S(t)oudt
Clin(t) Stoerner
Co(tt)on Davidson
Craig (M)or(t)on
Da(m)on Huard
Dan (F)ou(t)s
Danny Wuer(ff)el
Don (M)ajowski
Don (M)eride(t)h
Donovan (M)cNabb
Daryl La(m)onica
Doug (F)lu(t)ie
Earl (M)orall
(F)ran (T)arken(t)on
(F)rank Reich
(F)rankie Alber(t)
(F)rank (T)ripucka
George (M)ira
Gino (T)erra(t)a
Glenn (F)oley
Harry New(m)an
Hugh (M)illen
Jack (T)hompson
Jake Plu(mm)er
Jay (F)iedler
Je(ff) Blake
Je(ff) Garcia
Je(ff) George
Je(ff) Hos(t)e(t)ler
Je(ff) Ru(t)ledge
Ji(m) (F)inks
Ji(m) Harbaugh

Ji(m) Kelly
(Ji(m) (M)c(m)ahon
Ji(m) (M)iller
Ji(mm)y Conzel(m)an
Ji(m) Plunkett
Joe (F)erguson
Joe (M)on(t)ana
Joe Willie Na(m)a(t)h
John Ki(t)ner
John (M)cCor(m)ick
Johnny Uni(t)as
Jon Ki(t)na
Josh Boo(t)y
Ken(t) Graham
Kur(t) Warner
La(m)ar (M)cHan
(M)ark Brunell
(M)ark (M)alone
(M)ark Ripken
(M)ark Rypien
(M)ark Wilson
(M)arlin Briscoe
(M)arques (T)uiasosopo
(M)a(tt) Hasselbeck
(M)ax Choboain
(M)icheal Vicks
(M)icky Slaugh(t)er
(M)ike Livingston
(M)ike (M)c(M)ahon
(M)ike Pawlawski
(M)ike (T)omczak
(M)il(t)on Romney
Nor(m) Snead
Nor(m) Van Brocklin
O(tt)o Graham
Pay(t)on (M)anning
(P)hil Si(mm)s - p sounds to f
Ral(p)h (M)oss
Randy Wrigh(t)
Rick (M)ier
Rick (M)iller
Rodney Pee(t)e
Roger S(t)auback
Ryan Lea(f)
Sa(mm)y Baugh

Sco(tt) Hun(t)er
Sco(tt) (M)itchell
Sid Luck(m)an
S(t)eve Bono
S(t)eve Brokowski
S(t)eve DeBerg
S(t)eve (F)uller
S(t)eve (M)cNair
S(t)eve Ramsey
S(t)eve Ro(m)anik
S(t)eve Spurrier
S(t)eve (T)ensi
S(t)eve Young
(T)ed (M)archibroda
(T)ee (M)ar(t)in
(T)erry Bradshaw
(T)erry Hanra(tt)y
(T)i(m) Couch
(T)i(m) Ra(tt)ay
(T)obin Ro(t(e
(T)odd Bau(m)an
(T)odd Collins
(T)o(m) Brady
(T)o(m) (F)lores
(T)o(mm)y Kra(m)er
(T)o(mm)y (M)addux
(T)ravis Brown
(T)ravis (T)idwell
(T)ren(t) Dil(f)er
(T)ren(t)Green
(T)roy Aik(m)an
(T)y De(t)(m)er
Quincy Car(t)er
Vince (F)arraga(m)o
Vinnie (T)es(t)everde
Warren (M)oon
Y.A. (T)i(tt)le

Green Spiritual & Physical Center
Models:

A(m)y Wear
Alta (M)ota
Amber Valle(tt)a
Ana Bea(t)riz Barros
Annie (M)or(t)on
Anouk Ai(m)ee
A(t)hena Casino
Audrey (M)arnay
Aurore Cle(m)ent
Carla (M)aria
Car(m)en Kass
Carol Single(t)on
Carolyn (M)ur(p)y- (p)
sounds to f
Carrie (T)ivador
Cecilia Tho(m)sen
Chandra Nor(t)h
Cheryl (T)iegs
Chiann (F)an
Chris(t)y (T)urlington
Chris(t)y Brinkley
Chris(t)y Howell
Cindy (M)argolis
Cindy Craw(f)ord
Clare (M)awesa
Claudia Schi(ff)er
Da(m)on Willis
Diane Bu(m)ont
Ehrinn Cu(mm)ing
Elisa Beni(t)ez
Elle (M)acpherson
E(mm)anuelle Seigner
E(mm)e
Elle (M)acpherson
Es(t)elle Hallyday
Es(t)elle Warren
Es(t)her Canadus
(F)abio
(F)arrah Su(mm)er(f)ord
(F)elicia Swarez
Helena Chris(t)ensen
Isabeli (F)on(t)ana
I(m)an
Jean Shri(m)p(t)on
Jenni(f)er Corliss

Jenny (F)iller
Jere(m)y Black
Jill Su(mm)er
Josie (M)aran
Ka(t)ia Granina
Kadra Ah(m)ed O(m)an
Kahari (M)ays
Karen (M)aulder
Ki(m) Charl(t)on
Kris(t)ina Se(m)enovskaia
Lauren Hu(tt)on
Leann (T)weeden
Libby (M)atley
Lisa Kauff(m)an
Lisa (M)arie Sco(tt)
Lisa Schoon(m)aker
Lynn Su(t)herland
(M)aggie Rizer
(M)alia Jones
(M)arcus Schenkenberg
(M)arin Krull
(M)arisa (M)iller
(M)ark Vanderloo
(M)arlene Viegas
(M)arriane Sei(m)an
(M)aureen Gallhger
(M)elanie (T)hierry
(M)ellissa (M)cNight
(M)ichael Bengin
(M)ichelle Behennah
(M)ichikio
(M)ila Jones
(M)illa Jovovich
(M)olly Si(m)s
(M)orena Cornin
(M)uriel Andurand
(M)yka Dinkle
Na(t)alia Jovovich
Nao(m)i Campbell
Niki (T)aylor
Pa(t)rica Vasquez
Pe(t)ra Ne(m)cova
Rebbecca Ro(m)ijn Ra(m)os
Robert (M)onzi
S(t)e(ph)anie Sey(m)our - ph

sounds to f
Sa(ff)ron Aldridge
Sa(m)an(t)ha Jones
Sarah (T)homas
So(ph)ie Dahl
Stacy (M)cKenzie
Ste(ph)anie Roma(n)o(v) -
ph/v sounds to f
Ste(ph)anie Sey(m)our
Stella (T)ennat
(T)ara Caballero
(T)hao Nguyen
(T)i(ff)any Richardson
(T)ina Hebbelinck
(T)raci Bingham
(T)racy (T)rini(t)a
(T)rica Hel(f)er
(T)rish Goff
(T)wiggy
(T)yra Banks
(T)yson Beck(f)ord
Valeria (M)azza
Van(t)e Veronica
Wilhel(m)ina
Ya(m)ila Diaz Rahi
Yas(m)een Ghauri

Green Spiritual Center
Celebrities that have helped
Environmental Programs.

Bette (M)idler
(F)ay Dunaway
Jane (F)onda
(M)argo Kidder
(M)artin Sheen
(M)eryl Streep
(M)ike (F)arrell
(M)ickey Hart
(P)hil Donahue -(P) sounds
to (F)
Shirley (M)cClaine
(T)ed Dawson
(T)ed (T)urner
(T)imothy Bottoms

Green Spiritual Center Enviromentalists:

Claude (M)artin
Chico (M)endez
David (M)cTaggart
Dennis (M)eadows
Dianne (F)osse
Donna (M)eadows
Dr. (M)icheal (F)ay
Dr.(T)homas Eisner
Elizabeth (M)ay
(F)ritoof Capra
George (F)rampton
Henry David (T)horeau
Jerry (F)ranklin
Jerry (M)eral
Jim (F)owler
John (M)uir
(M)aneka Gandhi
(M)arjory Stoneman Douglas
(M)ark Chiyto
(M)ark Reisner
(M)arlin Perkins
(M)aurice Strong
(M)icheal Sutton
(M)ikeal (T)obais
(M)oshe Alamaro
(M)ustofa K. (T)olba
Rev. Danny (M)artin
Rev. (M)athew (F)ox
Rudy (M)endez
Russell (M)ittermeier
(T)ed Rubenstien
(T)homas Ballenstien
(T)homas (T)urner
(T)homas Wiess
Wangari (M)aathai

Green Spiritual Center Lawyers and Law Officials

(F)elix (F)urter
(F). Lee Bailey
(F)rancis Perkins
(M)arcia Clark
(M)arian Wright Edelman
(M)arvin (M)itchelson
(M)elvin Belli
(M)elvin Purvis
(T)heodore Roosevelt
(T)homas E. Dewey
(T)homas Jefferson
(T)hurgood (M)arshall
Edward (M)asry
Gov. (M)ario Coumo
Howard (T)aft
James (M)adison
John (M)arshall
Roger (T)aney

Green Spiritual Center Herbal Authors & Famous Healers:

Bob (F)laws
Chris (M)ead
Dorothy (M)orrison
Daniel B.(M)owery
Emeli (T)olley
Giavanni (M)aciocia
Jerry (T)raunfield
Louise (T)ennsey
(M)ark Blumenthal
(M)icheal (F)allon
(M)icheal (T)ierra
(M)ichael (T). (M)urray
(M)ichael Weiner
(M)ichelle Nostradamus
(M)ira Kaplan
(M)iranda Smith
(M)onica (M)oran
(M)onteen Gordon
(M)other (T)eresa
Steven (F)oster
(T)heresa Loe
(T)homas J. Edpel
(T)homas S. Elias

Famous Green Spiritual Center Peacemakers

Alfred Hermann (F)ried
Alva (M)yrdal
Auguste (M)arie (F)rancois Beernaert
Baroness Butha Sophie (F)elicita Von Sutter
Carlos (F)ilipe Ximenes Belo
David (T)rimble
Desmond (M)pilo (T)utu
Ernesto (T)eodoro (M)oneta
(F)erdinand Buisson
(F)rank Billings Kellogg
(F)rederic Passy
(F)rederik De Clerk
(F)redrik Bajer
(F)ridtjof Nansen
George Catlett (M)arshall
Henri La (F)ontaine
John Raleigh (M)ott
Le Duc (T)ho
(M)ahatma Gandhi
(M)airead Corrigan
(M)artin Luther King Jr.
(M)enachem Begin
(M)ikhail Sergeyevich Gorbachev
(M)ohamed Anwar Al Sadat
(M)other (T)heresa
Nee Countess Kinsky Von Chinic Uno (T)ettau

SAYINGS THAT STIMULATE GREEN SPIRITUAL PEOPLE:

Peace is the proper result of the Christian temper. It is the great kindness which our religion doth us, that it brings us to a settledness of mind, and a consistency within ourselves. - Bp. Patrick.

Peace is the happy, natural state of man: war, his corruption, his disgrace. - Thomson.

Peace is the golden wisp that binds the sheaf of blessings. - Katherine Lee Bates.

The alternative to peace is not war. It is annihilation. - Raymond Gram Swing.

Peace is the evening star of the soul, as virtue is its sun; and the two are never far apart. - Colton.

If we have not peace within ourselves it is vain to seek it from outward sources. - Rochefoucauld.

Peace is rarely denied to the peaceful. -Schiller.

The good need fear no law; it is his safety, and the bad man's awe. –Massinger.

Where law ends, tyranny begins. -Wm. Pitt.

Laws are the very bulwarks of liberties of all men. - J.G. Holland.

Laws are the silent assessors of God. - W.R. Alger.

The people's safety is the law of God. - James Otis.

BLUE SPIRITUAL PEOPLE

Blue spiritual people are those who's first, middle only if used regularly, or last names start with (G), (N), or (U), sounding letters. Blue is God's color of the spiritual, celestial, ethereal universe. It is God's spectrum of faith, imagination and soul color. Blue spiritual people are very imaginative, invent full, suave, soothing, soulful and spiritual. They have a natural sense of beauty, style and serenity. God's other key character attributes of this spectrum are: dependability, diplomacy (tactfulness), dutifulness, faithfulness, genius, meditative, open mindedness, spacious and spirited. The negative traits they need to guard against are: apathy, close mindedness, coldness, distrust, indiscretion, lack of faith, lack of spirit, laziness, superstitious, tactlessness and undependability. The blue spectrum consists of light baby blues, sky blues, true hue blue, royal blues, navy blues and dark midnight blues. Your favorite spiritual center colors will look and feel very cheerful, clean, creative, happy, imaginative, moral, spacious, spirited and wholesome, on and around you. Use your spiritual center colors to create these images and feelings in your wardrobe and home-decor. Go to the color fans in the photo section of the book and determine your favorite blue spiritual center colors, then go to the 3-part chart in the back of the book and record them.

NATURAL CAREER CHOICES THAT BLUE SPIRITUAL PEOPLE EXCEL IN:

Famous Inventors:

Alexander (G)raham Bell
Alfred (N)oble
Charles (G)oodyear
Charon Robin (G)anellin
Edmund (G)umer
Elisha (G)raves Otis
E(u)gene Houdry - E is silent
(G) alileo (G)alilei
(G)arrett A. Morgan
(G)erhard M. Sessler
(G)ertrude Belle
(G)ordon (G)ould
(G)race Hopper
(G)raham John Durant
(G)ranville T. Woods
(G)uglielmo Marconi
Julius (N)ieuwland
Lenard Michael (G)reene
(N)icholas Copernicus
(N)icholaus August Otto
(N)ikola Tesla
John (N)apier
John (N)oble
Joseph (N)icephore
Robert Hutchings (G)oddard
Robert (N)(N)oyce
Sir Isaac (N)ewton
Thomas (N)ewcomen
Wilson (G)reatbatch

Famous Blue Spiritual Stylist/Designers:

Charles (N)olan
Comme De(G)arlos
Dries Van (N)oten
(G)abrielle Coco Chanel
(G)eoffrey Bean
(G)ilbert Adrian
(G)illes Dufour
(G)ivenchy
(G)loria Vanderbilt
(G)ucci
Jacques (G)arcia
James (G)alanos
John (G)alliano
Mark (G)rant
(N)arcisco Rodrique
(N)at Taylor
(N)ick (G)raham
(N)icole Farhi
(N)olan Miller
(N)orman (N)orell
Pierre (G)arroudi
Rudy (G)ernreich

SAYINGS THAT STIMULATE BLUE SPIRITUAL PEOPLE:

Faith makes the discords of the present the harmonies of the future. - Collyer

Artists treat facts as stimuli for imagination, whereas scientists use imagination to coordinate facts. - Arthur Koestler

An uncommon degree of imagination constitutes poetical genius. - Dugald Stewart

Either we have an immortal soul or we have not. If we have not, we are beasts; the first and wisest of beasts it may be; but still beasts. We only differ in degree, and not in kind; just as the elephant differs from the slug. But by the concession of the materialists, we are not of the same kind as beasts; and this also we say from our own consciousness. Therefore, me think, it must be the possession of a soul within us that makes the difference. - Coleridge

The body, that is but dust; the soul, it is a bud of eternity. - N. Culverwell

Faith makes all evil good to us, and all good better; unbelief makes all good evil, and all evil worse. Faith laughs at the shaking of the spear; unbelief trembles at the shaking of a leaf, unbelief starves the soul; faith finds food in famine, and a table in the wilderness. In the greatest danger, faith says, "I have a great God."

When outward strength is broken, faith rests on the promises. In the midst of sorrow, faith draws the sting out of every trouble, and takes out the bitterness from every affliction. - Cecil

Science has sometimes been said to be opposed to faith, and inconsistent with it. - But all science, in fact, rests on a basis of faith, for it assumes the permanence and uniformity of natural laws - a thing which can never be demonstrated. - Tryon Edwards

The human race built most nobly when limitations were greatest and therefore, when most was required of imagination in order to build at all. Limitations seem to have always been the best friends of architecture. - Frank Lloyd Wright

It is the divine attribute of the imagination, that when the real world is shut out it can create a world for itself, and with a necromantic power can conjure up glorious shapes and forms, and brilliant visions to make solitude populous, and irradiate the gloom of a dungeon.
- Washington Irving

The problem of restoring to the world original and eternal beauty is solved by the redemption of the soul. - Emerson

It seems to me as if not only the form but the soul of man was made to walk erect and look upon the stars.- Bulwer

The steps of faith fall on the seeming void, but find the rock beneath. - Whittier

The soul without imagination is what an observatory would be without a telescope.
- H.W. Beecher

The human soul is like a bird that is born in a cage. Nothing can deprive it of its natural long-ings, or obliterate the mysterious remembrance of its heritage. - Epes Sargent

To look upon the soul as going on from strength to strength, to consider that she is to shine for-ever with new eternity, that she will be still adding virtue to virtue, and knowledge to knowledge; carries in it something wonderfully agreeable to that ambition which is natural to the mind of man. - Addison

Faith is the root of all good works; a root that produces nothing is dead. - Daniel Wilson

The faculty of imagination is the great spring of human activity, and the principal source of human improvement. As it delights in presenting to the mind, scenes and characters more per-fect than those which we are acquainted with, it prevents us from ever being completely satis-fied with our present condition, or with our past attainments, and engages us continually in the pursuit of some untried enjoyment, or of some ideal excellence. Destroy this faculty, and the condition of man will become as stationary as that of the brutes. - Dugold Stewart

The wealth of a soul is measured by how much it can feel, and its poverty by how little.
- W.R. Alger

I am fully convinced that the soul is indestructible, and that its activity will continue through eter-nity. It is like the sun, which, to our eyes, seems to set in night; but it has in reality only gone to diffuse its light elsewhere. - Goethe

To believe is to be strong. Doubt cramps energy. Belief is power. - F.W. Robertson

Imagination disposes of everything; it creates beauty, justice, and happiness, which are every-thing in this world. - Pascal

Heaven-born, the soul a heavenward course must hold; beyond the world she soars; the wise man, I affirm, can find no rest in that which perishes, nor will he lend his heart to aught that doth on time depend. - Michael Angelo

When men cease to be faithful to their God, he who expects to find them so to each other will be much disappointed. - George Horne

The human mind cannot create anything. It produces nothing until after having been fertilized by experience and meditation; its acquisitions are the germs of its production. - Buffon

Narrow minds think nothing right that is above their own capacity. - Rochefoucauld

The saddest of all failures is that of a soul, with its capabilities and possibilities, failing of life everlasting, and entering on that night of death upon which no morning ever dawns.
- Herrick Johnson

There are few who need complain of the narrowness of their minds if they will only do their best with them. - Hobbes

Life is the soul's nursery - its training place for the destinies of eternity. - Thackeray

Chapter 5

YOUR MENTAL CENTER COLORS, TRAITS AND TALENTS

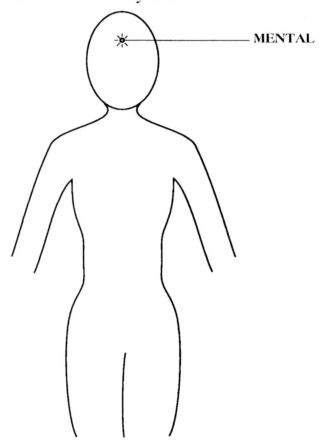

Mental Center
Middle Forehead
Between Eyebrows

Your mental center is located at the middle of your forehead at your eyebrow level, in the area of your pituitary gland and the area eastern philosophies call the brow chakra. Your mental center is where your analytical, common sense, intellectual, logical, mental personality and skills originate. The letters that determine your mental center colors, character traits and talents are the second sounding letters in your first, (middle only if used regularly) and last names. For example: S(a)ndy W(i)lson is a flesh and purple mental center color person. Check the color-letter chart on page 25 to see what your mental center colors are, then go to the preceding mental/color sections in this chapter and see what your mental center colors say about you. Then go to the back of the book and record your mental center colors in the three-part chart. (If both your mental center color letters are attuned to the same color spectrum then you are a double mental color person, which would make that particular color spectrum to have a very strong influencing affect on your mental center).

Those that cultivate and operate off of this center are the analytical, intellectual, and logical type. Classic examples would be: a computer analyst, doctors, lawyers, mathematicians, professors, scientists, and those who have used good common sense to achieve their goals. Those who do not cultivate this center will continually lack good common sense and intellectual skills. Your mental center colors will feel and look intellectual, practical, and studious, on and around you. Your mental center colors that you use in wardrobe and home or business decor should be non-flashy in texture and design such as cottons, gabardines, linens, oxfords, wool's (chevrons, hounds tooth, knits, plaids, tweeds etc). To learn the basic steps to cultivate your mental center read chapter 28.

FLESH MENTAL CENTER PEOPLE

Flesh mental center people are those whose second sounding letters in their first, middle only if used regularly, and last names are (A), (H), (O) or (V) letters. The positive or negative character attributes of the flesh spectrum, depending on which ones you cultivate, will be the way in which you project mentally. The positive are: articulateness, cleanliness, compensation, coordination, harmony, introspective, memory recall, morality, organization, practicality, perception, unity (mind-body-soul), and universality. The negative character traits are: confusion, disorderliness, filthiness, forgetfulness, immorality, idolatry, inarticulate, inconsiderateness, inconsistency, lacking coordination, inharmonious, impractical.

Your favorite mental center colors will look intelligent, logical and practical on and around you. Use your mental center colors in your wardrobe and home-decor to create these images and feelings. You could use your mental center colors in your wardrobe to create an intellectual image or in your home-decor in a study room to stimulate yourself intellectually. The flesh spectrum ranges from off whites, beige's, tans, light browns, browns, dark browns and dark chocolate browns. Go to the color fan in the photo section of this book and determine your favorite flesh spectrum colors. Then go to your 3-part chart in the back of the book and record them.

PURPLE MENTAL CENTER PEOPLE

Purple mental center people are those whose second sounding letters in their first, (middle only if used regularly), or last names are (B), (I), (P), or (W), sounding letters. For example: J(i)ll Jones or another example, Sandy S(p)arks. If both of your names have a second sounding purple letter then you would be a double purple mental person, example: B(i)ll W(i)lliams. Depending on whether a person cultivates the positive or negative traits of the purple spectrum attributes will determine their mental center personality and talents. The positive traits are: civilized, cultured, dedicated, dignified, empowered, idealistic, intuitive, loyal, mature, regal, self-sacrificing and tasteful.

The negative traits are: domination, fanaticism lack of taste, monopolization, pompousness, pettiness, snobbishness, superiority, treachery, uncivilized, and undignified.

Your favorite mental center colors will look intelligent, logical and practical on and around you. Use your mental center colors in your wardrobe and home-decor to create these images and feelings. You could use your mental center colors in your wardrobe to create an intellectual image or in a study room to stimulate yourself intellectually. The purple spectrum ranges from light lavenders, true hue purples and deep violets. Go to the color fan in the photo section of this book and determine your favorite purple spectrum colors. Then go to the back of the book and record them in your 3- part chart.

RED MENTAL CENTER PEOPLE

Red mental center people are those whose second sounding letters in their first, (middle only if used regularly), or last names are (C), (J), (Q), or (X) sounding letters. For example: B. (J) Jones. Depending on whether a person cultivates the positive or negative traits of the red spectrum attributes will determine their red mental center personality and talents. The positive character attributes of the red spectrum are: beauty of manner (elegance), benevolence (sense of good will), charitableness, chivalry, compassion, courteous (mercifulness), gracefulness, gratefulness (thankfulness), honesty (sincerity), persistence (tenaciousness), physical life energy, romance and valor, (courage). The negative traits of the red spectrum are: brutality, dishonesty, excessive carnal desire, impulsiveness (impatience), jealousy (envy), physical egotism, physical laziness, pitilessness (lack of compassion), rudeness (coarseness), savageness (barbaric).

Your favorite mental center colors will look intelligent, logical and practical on and around you. Use your mental center colors in your wardrobe and home-decor to create these images and feelings. You could use your mental center colors in your wardrobe to create an intellectual image or a study room to stimulate yourself intellectually. The Red spectrum consists of pink reds, rose reds, true hue reds, cranberry reds and dark wine reds. Go to the color fan in the photo section of this book and determine your favorite red spectrum colors.

ORANGE MENTAL CENTER PEOPLE

Orange mental center people are those whose second sounding letters in their first, middle only if used regularly, or last names are (D), (K), (R), or (Y) sounding letters. For example: E(d)ward Jones or Nancy E(d)monds. The positive character traits of the orange spectrum are: affection (fondness), creativity, inspirational enthusiasm, joyfulness, kindness (warm heartedness), repentance, self-assurance, speculation, venturesome, and versatility. The negative traits are: boastfulness, despair (depression), destructiveness, exhibitionism, flamboyance and unpleas-antness.

Your favorite mental center colors will look intelligent, logical and practical on and around you. Use your mental center colors in your wardrobe and home-decor to create these images and feelings. You could use your mental center colors in your wardrobe to create an intellectual image or in a study room to stimulate yourself intellectually. The orange spectrum ranges from the light peaches, light corals, true hue orange, rust and dark earthy rust oranges. Go to the color fan in the photo section of this book and determine your favorite orange spectrum colors. Then record them in your 3-part chart in the back of the book.

YELLOW MENTAL CENTER PEOPLE

Yellow mental center people are those whose second sounding letters in their first, middle only if used regularly, or last names are (E), (L), (S), or (Z). For example: D(e)bbie Long or Candy G(l)eason. Yellow is the intellectual and analytical color. It is also the positive thinking, cheerful and optimistic spectrum. God's other positive character attributes of this spectrum are, clarity, comprehension, decisiveness, glorification (of God), logic, and reasonableness. Here are the negative character traits: conniving, deception, pessimism, shrewdness and vindictiveness.

Your favorite mental center colors will look intelligent, logical and practical on and around you. Use your mental center colors in your wardrobe and home-decor to create these images and feelings. You could use your mental center colors in your wardrobe to create a intellectual image or in a study room to stimulate yourself intellectually. The yellow spectrum consists of the light pale yellow's, true hue yellow, gold yellow's and dark copper yellow's. Go to the color fan in the photo section of this book and determine your favorite yellow spectrum colors. Then record them in your 3- part chart at the back of the book.

GREEN MENTAL CENTER PEOPLE

Green mental center people are those whose second sounding letters in their first, middle only if used regularly, or last names are (F), (M), or (T). For example: S(t)ella Carson or Brandy S(m)ith. Green is God's spectrum of balance, control (self-control), and peacefulness. The other positive traits of the green spectrum are, caution, cooperation, critical, discrimination, equi-tableness (agreeableness), impartiality (fairness), lawfulness, and poise. The negative traits are: bias, callousness, disagreeableness, envy, lack of judgment, miserliness, sense of injustice, and suspicion.

Your favorite mental center colors will look intelligent, logical and practical on and around you. Use your mental center colors in your wardrobe and home-decor to create these images and feelings. You could use your mental center colors in your wardrobe to create an intellectual image or in a study room to stimulate yourself intellectually. The green spectrum ranges from light mint green, true hue green to dark forest green. Go to the color fan in the photo section of this book and determine your favorite green spectrum colors. Then record them in your 3-part chart at the back of the book.

BLUE MENTAL CENTER PEOPLE

Blue mental center people are those whose second sounding letters in their first, middle only if used regularly, or last names are (G), (N), or (U). For example: A(n)nette Fong or Gina N(u)mon. The positive traits of the blue spectrum are: dependability, diplomacy (tactfulness), dutifulness, faithfulness, genius, meditative, open-mindedness, sense of beauty, spacious, and spirited. The negative traits are: apathy, close mindedness, coldness, distrust, indiscretion, lack of faith, lack of spirit, laziness, superstitious, tactlessness and undependability.

Your favorite mental center colors will look intelligent, logical and practical on and around you. Use your mental center colors in your wardrobe and home-decor to create these images and feelings. You could use your mental center colors in your wardrobe to create an intellectual image or in a study room to stimulate yourself intellectually. The blue spectrum consists of light baby blues, sky blues, true hue blue, royal blues, navy blues and dark midnight blues. Go to the color fan in the photo section of this book and determine your favorite blue spectrum colors. Then record them in your 3-part chart in the back of the book.

Chapter 6

YOUR VOCAL CENTER COLORS, TRAITS AND TALENTS

Vocal Center
Base of Throat

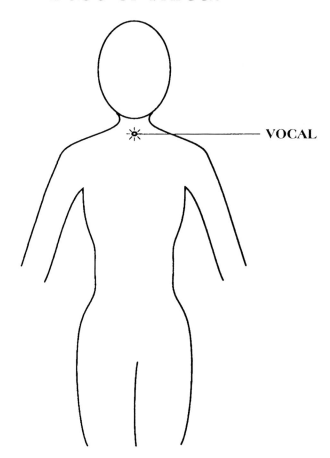

VOCAL

Your vocal center is located at the base of your throat, in the same area as your thyroid endocrine gland. Eastern philosophies refer to this area as the throat chakra center. The vocal center functions are: your vocal communications center for speaking, harmony center for singing (check out the orange vocal center section to see how 70% or more of the most famous singers are orange vocal center people because of the main orange character attribute trait of creativity), and your center for diplomatic harmonious relationships with others including yourself and your unity (spirit, body, soul) organizing center. This is the center that, when we are functioning correctly, will give us the overall feeling of being in complete harmony, spirit, body and soul, or as some say mind, body and soul, or simply when everything is pleasantly organized and going well in our lives. Classic examples of those that cultivate and operate off of their vocal center are: articulate, diplomats, singers, speakers, ventriloquist's, voice imitators, and people who always seem to be harmonious and hardly ever seem to argue with others. Vocal center people usually are very neat and organized.

Name Colorology could be used in personal and worldly diplomatic situations, for example: take two countries sending diplomats to try to solve different problems between these countries. They would probably have a much higher success rate of understanding and agreeableness if they would both send diplomats that had the same harmony center colors and other center similarities.

The letters in your names that determine your vocal center colors, traits, and talents are the third sounding letters in your first, middle only if used regularly, and last name. For example: Sa(n)dy Ba(k)er, looking at the letter-color chart on page 25 you would see this person is a blue and orange vocal center person. Looking at the letter-color chart, determine your vocal center colors, and then go to the following vocal center color sections to find out your specific vocal center traits and talents. After doing all of the above go to the 3-part chart in the back of the book and record your vocal center colors. To learn the basic steps to cultivate your vocal center read chapter 28. Use materials that have very harmonious, neat, and organized lines, patterns, and textures for your vocal center colors.

FLESH VOCAL CENTER PEOPLE

Flesh vocal center people are those whose third sounding letters in their first, middle only if used regularly, or last names are (A), (H), (O), or (V). For example: Di(a)na Richards, El(v)is Presley or Rebecca Gr(a)y. The positive or negative character attributes of the flesh spectrum (depending on which ones you cultivate) will be the way in which you project harmoniously. The positive are: articulateness, cleanliness, compensation, coordination, harmony, introspective, memory recall, morality, organization, practicality, perception, unity (mind-body-soul), and universality. The negative character traits are, confusion, disorderliness, filthiness, forgetfulness, immorality, idolatry, inarticulate, inconsiderateness, inconsistency, lacking coordination, inharmonious, and impracticality.

Your vocal center colors will look and feel very conversational, coordinated, harmonious, pleasant, neat and organized. Use your vocal center colors in your wardrobe and home-decor to create these images and feelings. The flesh spectrum ranges from off whites, beige's, tans, light browns, browns, dark browns and dark chocolate browns. Go to the color fan in the photo section of this book and determine your favorite flesh spectrum colors and then record them in your 3-part chart.

PURPLE VOCAL CENTER PEOPLE

Purple vocal center people are those who have the third sounding letters of (B), (I), (P), or (W), in their first, middle only if used regularly, or last names. For example: Re(b)ecca Long or June Ro(p)er. If you are a purple vocal center person the way you will project vocally/harmoniously will depend if you cultivate the positive or negative traits of this spectrum. The positive traits are: civilized, cultured, dedicated, dignified, empowered, idealistic, intuitive, loyal, mature, regal, self-sacrificing and tasteful.

Their negative traits are, domination, fanaticism, lack of taste, monopolization, pompousness, pettiness, snobbishness, superiority, treachery, uncivilized, and undignified.

Your vocal center colors will stimulate, look and feel conversational, coordinated, harmonious, pleasant, neat and organized, on and around you. Use your vocal center colors in your wardrobe and home-decor to create these images and feelings. The purple spectrum ranges from light lavenders, true hue purple and deep violets. Go to the color fan in the photo section of this book and determine your favorite purple spectrum colors, then record them in your 3-part chart in the back of the book.

RED VOCAL CENTER PEOPLE

Red vocal center people are those whose third sounding letters in their first, middle only if used regularly, or last names are (C), (J), (Q), or (X). For example: An(g)el Wright (the g in her first name sounds to j) or Sandy Mo(j)as. If you are a red vocal center person the way you will project vocally/harmoniously will depend if you cultivate the positive or negative traits of this spectrum. The positive traits are, beauty of manner (elegance), benevolence (sense of good will), charitableness, chivalry, compassion, courteous (mercifulness), gracefulness, gratefulness (thankfulness), honesty (sincerity), persistence (tenaciousness), physical life energy, romance, and valor (courage). The negative traits of the red spectrum are, brutality, dishonesty, excessive carnal desire, impulsiveness (impatience), jealousy (envy), physical egotism, physical laziness, pitilessness (lack of compassion), rudeness (coarseness), savageness (barbaric).

Your vocal center colors will stimulate, look and feel conversational, coordinated, harmonious, pleasant, neat and organized, on and around you. Use your vocal center colors in your wardrobe and home-decor to create these images and feelings. The red spectrum consists of pink reds, rose reds, true hue red, cranberry reds and dark wine reds. Go to the color fans in the photo section of this book and determine your favorite red spectrum colors.

ORANGE VOCAL CENTER PEOPLE

Orange vocal center people are those whose third sounding letters in their first, middle only if used regularly, or last names are (D), (K), (R), or (Y). For example: Ma(r)iah Ca(r)ey , Ba(r)bara Lewis or Ma(r)io Lanza. 70% or higher of the most famous singers are orange vocal center people-look at the list in this section. If you are an orange vocal center person the way you will project vocally/harmoniously will depend if you cultivate the positive or negative traits of this spectrum. The positive character traits of the orange spectrum are: affection (fondness), creativity, inspirational enthusiasm, joyfulness, kindness (warm heartedness), repentance, self-assurance, speculation, venturesome, versatile. The negative traits are, boastfulness, despair (depression), destructiveness, exhibitionism, flamboyance and unpleasantness. Your vocal center colors will stimulate, look, and feel conversational, coordinated, harmonious, pleasant, neat, and organized on and around you. Use your vocal center colors in your wardrobe and home-decor to create these images and feelings. The orange spectrum ranges from the light peaches, light corals, true hue orange, rust and dark earthy rust oranges. Go to the color fan in the photo section of this book and determine your favorite orange spectrum colors.

ORANGE VOCAL CENTER SINGERS

 I attribute the high percentage of famous orange vocal center singers to the main character traits of the orange spectrum of creativity and versatility to this phenomenon. So to put it simply these people are very creative and versatile from their vocal center because they have orange attuned to this center.

Orange Spectrum - Creativity - Kindness - Versatility
(D, K, R, Y)*   *c's may sound to K   *ia may sound to Y   *tt may sound to dd
Orange Vocal Center
Famous Singers:

Aa(r)on Neville	An(d)y Kim	Art Ja(r)rett
AJ M(c)lean	An(d)y Pa(r)tridge	Ava Ba(r)ber
Alanis Mo(r)issette	An(d)y Russell	Ba(r)bara Ann Haw(k)ins
Al(d)ridge Sisters	An(d)y Williams	Ba(r)bara Fai(r)child
Alejandro Fe(r)nandez	Angelo Moo(r)e	Ba(r)bara Geo(r)ge
Al Ja(r)dine	Angie Ma(r)tinez	Ba(r)bara Hendricks
Al Ja(rr)eau	Anita Bo(y)er	Ba(r)bara Lee
Al Ma(r)tino	Anita Wa(r)d	Ba(r)bara Lewis
Ana Ba(r)bara	Ann Bu(r)ton	Ba(r)bara Mason
An(d)rea Bocelli	Anne Mu(r)ray	Ba(r)bara St(r)iesand
An(d)rea Gruber	Annie Ma(r)ie Moss	Ba(r)rett St(r)ong
An(d)res Calamaro	Art Ca(r)ney	Ba(r)ry Gibb
An(d)rew Sisters	Art Ga(r)funkel	Ba(r)ry Manilow
An(d)y Gibb	Ar(t)ie Shaw	Ba(r)ry Sa(d)ler

Ba(r)ry White
Bar(r)y M(c)Guire
Belinda Ca(r)lisle
Be(r)t Bacharach
Be(r)tie Higgins
Bette Mi(d)ler
Be(t)ty Bonney
Be(t)ty Bradley
Be(t)ty Brewer
Be(t)ty Ca(r)ter
Be(t)ty Claire
Be(t)ty Clooney
Be(t)ty Engels
Be(t)ty Everette
Be(t)ty Grable
Be(t)ty Hutton
Be(t)ty No(r)ton
Be(t)ty Roche
Be(t)ty Van
Be(t)ty Wright
Bill An(d)erson
Bobby Ba(r)e
Bobby Ba(r)i
Bobby Da(r)rin
Bobby M(c)Farrin
Bobby Ry(d)ell
Bob Ca(r)roll
Bob Go(d)ay
Bob Li(d)o
Bob Ma(r)ley
Bob M(c)Coy
Bo Di(d)dley
Boo(k)er T. Jones
Bonnie La(k)e
Bo(r)is Block
Bryan A(d)ams
Brian M(c)Night
Bruce Sp(r)ingstein
Bryan Ab(r)ams
Bryan Fe(r)ris
Bryn Te(r)fel
Bu(c)k Owens
Bu(d)dy Clark
Bu(d)dy De Vi(t)o
Bu(d)dy Gately
Bu(d)dy Greco
Bu(d)dy Holly

Bu(d)dy Hughes
Bu(d)dy Stewart
Bu(d)dy Welcome
Ca(r)l Ca(r)lton
Ca(r)l Denny
Ca(r)l Douglas
Ca(r)la Thomas
Ca(r)los Valdez
Ca(r)los Vives
Ca(r)lotta Dale
Ca(r)ly Simon
Ca(r)men Bradford
Ca(r)men Lombardo
Ca(r)men M(c)Rae
Ca(r)men Mi(r)anda
Ca(r)ole King
Ca(r)ol Kaye
Ca(r)ol Ma(c)kay
Ca(r)ol Sloane
Ca(r)olyn Gray
Cecilia Ba(r)toli
Celine Ma(r)ie Dion
Chichi Pe(r)alta
Ch(r)is Conners
Ch(r)is Ki(r)kpatrick
Ch(r)istina Aguilera
Ch(r)istopher Cross
Cha(r)lie Pride
Cha(r)lie Rich
Chet At(k)ins
Chuck Be(r)ry
Chuck Ja(c)kson
Claire Ma(r)tin
Cla(r)a Wa(r)el
Cla(r)ence Ca(r)ter
Clark Yo(c)um
Clyde Bu(r)ke
Clyde M(c)Phatter
Clyde Ro(d)gers
Co(r)nelius Bros.
Co(r)y Ha(r)t
Cu(r)t Ramsey
Cu(r)tis Mayfield
Cu(r)tis Stigers
C.W. M(c)coll
Dan Ha(r)tman
Danny Woo(d)

Da(r)ren Hayes
Da(r)yl Ryce
Da(r)yl Singletary
Danny Woo(d)
Dave Du(d)ley
Dean Ma(r)tin
Deanna Du(r)bin
Debra Ha(r)ry
Delores Ma(r)tel
Di(c)k Dale
Di(c)k Dyer
Di(c)k Ha(r)ding
Di(c)k Haynes
Di(c)k Me(r)rick
Di(c)k To(d)d
Di(c)k Webster
Di(d)o
Dolly Pa(r)ton
Dolores Do(d)ie ONeill
Dolores Haw(k)ins
Domenico Mo(d)ugno
Don Co(r)nell
Don Ha(r)tman
Don Mc(C)lean
Donna Fa(r)go
Do(r)is Day
Do(r)is Robbins
Do(r)is Troy
Do(r)othy Allen
Do(r)othy Claire
Do(r)othy Collins
Do(r)othy Dunn
Do(r)othy No(r)wood
Do(r)sey An(d)erson
Do(r)thy Danridge
Do(t)tie Evans
Du(k)e Ellington
Dusty Sp(r)ingfield
Ea(r)l Grant
Ea(r)l Wa(r)ren
E(r)ic Ca(r)men
E(r)os Ramazzotti
Ed(d)ie Arnold
Ed(d)ie Co(c)hran
Ed(d)ie Fisher
Ed(d)ie Floyd
Ed(d)ie Grant

Ed(d)ie Holland
Ed(d)ie Holman
Ed(d)ie Howard
Ed(d)ie Money
Ed(d)ie Rabbit
Ed(d)ie Stone
Ed(d)y Arnold
Ede Ca(r)le
Edie A(d)ams
Ella Mae Mo(r)se
Elvis Aa(r)on Presley
Emmy Lou Ha(r)ris
Em(r)ie Ann Lincoln
En(r)ico Ca(r)ruso
En(r)ique Iglesias
En(y)a
Eric Bu(r)den
Eric Ca(r)men
Eric Ca(r)ter
Eriko Sa(k)amoto
Ernestine An(d)erson
Ethel Me(r)man
Eugenie Bai(r)d
Eydie Go(r)me
Fa(r)on Young
Fe(r)lin Husky
Flora Pu(r)im
Fo(r)d Lea(r)y
Frankie Fo(r)d
Fran Wa(r)ren
Freddie Ja(c)kson
Freddie Ja(c)kson
Freddie Me(r)cury
Gail Fa(r)rell
Gale Ga(r)nett
Ga(r)net Mimms
Ga(r)th Brooks
Ga(r)y Johns
Ga(r)y Lewis
Ga(r)y Stevens
Ga(r)y Stewart
Ga(r)y U.S. Bonds
Ga(r)y Wright
Gene M(c)Daniels
Gene Me(r)lino
Geo(r)ge Benson
Geo(r)ge Brandon

Geo(r)ge Hamilton
Geo(r)ge Ha(r)rison
Geo(r)ge Jones
Geo(r)ge M(c)Corkle
Geo(r)ge Mi(c)hael
Geo(r)ge Tunnell
Geo(r)gia Ca(r)rol
Geo(r)gia Gibbs
Glenn Ya(r)borough
Gloria Es(t)avan (t) is pro-
nounced as a (d)
Gloria Ha(r)t
Gloria Woo(d)
Go(r)don Drake
Go(r)don Lightfoot
Go(r)don Ma(c)al
Go(r)don Ma(c)rae
Greg La(k)e
Gussippe Ve(r)di
Hal De(r)win
Hank Lo(c)klin
Ha(r)old Melvin
Ha(r)ry Belafonte
Ha(r)ry Mills
Ha(r)vey Fuqoua
Hank Lo(c)klin
Ha(r)old Arlen
Ha(r)riet Clark
Ha(r)riet Hilliard
Ha(r)ry Babbitt
Ha(r)ry Ba(r)nes
Ha(r)ry Brooks
Ha(r)ry Cool
Ha(r)ry Nilsson
Ha(r)ry Von Zell
Har(r)y Wa(y)ne Casey
He(r)b Albert
He(r)b Fame
He(r)b Jeffries
He(r)b Mills
Helen Fo(rr)est
Helen Me(rr)ill
Helen Re(d)dy
Helen Wa(r)d
Hoagy Ca(r)michael
Howard Goo(d)man
Howie Do(r)ough

Hu(d)die Lea(d)better
(Lea(d) Belly)
Ike Tu(r)ner
In(d)ia .Arie
Irene Ca(r)a
Ivan Pa(r)ker
Ivie An(d)erson
Ja(c)i Valesquez
Ja(c)k Ca(r)roll
Ja(c)k Daniels
Ja(c)k De France
Ja(c)k Fulton
Ja(c)k Greene
Ja(c)k Haskell
Ja(c)k Hunter
Ja(c)k Lathrop
Ja(c)k Leonard
Ja(c)ki Cooper
Ja(c)kie Deshannon
Ja(c)kie Ho(r)ne
Ja(c)kie Wilson
Ja(c)k Ingram
Ja(c)k Jones
Ja(c)kson Browne
Ja(c)k Wagner
Ja(c)ob Dillion
Ja(k)e Hess
James Da(r)ren
Jane Ha(r)vey
Janie Fo(r)d
Jean El(d)ridge
Je(r)i Southern
Je(r)ome Jones
Je(r)ry Browne
Je(r)ry Butler
Je(r)ry Ma(r)sten
Je(r)ry Ree(d)
Je(r)ry Stuart
Je(r)ry Vale
Jesse Di(c)kson
Jesse No(r)man
Jessica An(d)rews
Jimmie Ro(d)gers
Jo (D)ee Messina
Jo(d)y Watley
Jo(r)don Knight
Joe Co(c)ker

Joe M(c)Intyre
Joesph Ga(r)lington
John An(d)erson
John Fo(r)d Coley
John M(c)Afee
Johnny Bu(r)nette
Johnny Da(r)cy
Johnny Ho(r)ton
Johnny Me(r)cer
Jon An(d)erson
Jon Se(c)ada
Jose Ca(r)reras
Josephine Ba(k)er
Jo(y)a Sherrill
Jr. Wal(k)er
Ju(d)y Collins
Ju(d)y Ga(r)land
Ju(d)y Starr
Julie An(d)rews
June Ch(r)isty
Ka(rr)in Allyson
Kay Ca(r)lton
Kay Li(t)tle
Kenny Ga(r)dner
Kenny Ma(r)tin
Kenny Sa(r)gent
Kim Ca(r)nes
Ki(r)i Te Kanawa
Ki(r)k Franklin
Ki(t)ty Allen
Ki(t)ty Kallen
Ki(t)ty Lane
Kristin He(r)sh
La(r)ry Cotton
La(r)ry Douglas
La(r)ry Gatlin
La(r)ry Hopper
La(r)ry Southern
La(r)ry Taylor
Lau(r)a Fygi
Lau(r)a Pausini
Lau(r)eano Brizuela
Lau(r)yn Hill
Laverne Ba(k)er
Leif Ga(r)rett
Le(r)oy Van Dy(k)e
Len Ba(r)ry

Lesley Go(r)e
Lilly Ann Ca(r)ol
Li(t)tle Eva
Li(t)tle Richard
Liza Mo(r)row
Lo(r)e(tt)a Lynn
Lo(r)eena M(c)Kennitt
Lo(r)ez Alexandria
Lo(r)raine Benson
Lo(r)rie Mo(r)gan
Louis En(r)ique
Louis Jo(r)dan
Lucille Do(r)an
Lucy Ree(d)
Lyn An(d)erson
Lynn An(d)erson
Lynn Ba(r)i
Mabel Me(r)cer
Ma(c) Davis
M(c)Quire Sisters
Ma(d)onna Ci(c)cone
Mandy Moo(r)e
Ma(r)c Anthony
Ma(r)garet M(c)Crae
Ma(r)garet Whiting
Ma(r)gie Woo(d)
Ma(r)ie Milldour
Ma(r)ia Beltran Ruiz
Ma(r)ia (C)allas
Ma(r)iah Ca(r)ey
Ma(r)ianne Faithful
Ma(r)ian Thompson
Ma(r)ie Ellington
Ma(r)ie Hutton
Ma(r)ie Osmond
Ma(r)ilyn Du(k)e
Ma(r)ilyn Ho(r)ne
Ma(r)ilyn Maxwell
Ma(r)ilyn Mc(C)oo
Ma(r)ion Ca(r)ol
Ma(r)ion Hutton
Ma(r)ion Mann
Ma(r)jorie Hughes
Ma(r)k Dinning
Ma(r)k Eitzel
Ma(r)k Lowrey

Ma(r)k Miller
Ma(r)k Nesler
Ma(r)k Willis
Ma(r)lena Shaw
Ma(r)lene Ver Planck
Ma(r)ni Nixon
Ma(r)shall Crenshaw
Ma(r)tha Bass
Ma(r)tha Rae
Ma(r)tha Reeves
Ma(r)tie Sa(r)del
Ma(r)tha Tilton
Ma(r)tha Wayne
Ma(r)tina M(c)Bride
Ma(r)ty M(c)Kenna
Ma(r)ty Robbins
Ma(r)v Johnson
Ma(r)vin Gaye
Ma(r)y Ann M(c)All
Ma(r)y Chapin Ca(r)penter
Ma(r)y Costa
Ma(r)y Dugan
Ma(r)y Fo(r)d
Ma(r)yilyn Moo(r)e
Ma(r)y Lou Lo(r)o
Ma(r)y Lou Metzer
Ma(r)y Ma(r)tin
Ma(r)y Spears
Ma(r)y Stallings
Ma(r)y Travers
Ma(r)y Wells
Ma(r)ylyn Ho(r)ne
Mau(r)ice Williams
Mau(r)y Cross
Me(r)edith Brooks
Me(r)le Haggart
Mel To(r)me
Melinda Ca(r)slile
Me(r)edith Blake
Me(r)edith d' Ambrosio
Me(r)v Griffen
Me(r)wyn Bogue
Mi(c)hael Assante
Mi(c)hael Author
Mi(c)hael Bolton
Mi(c)hael Co(r)s
Mi(c)hael Feinstein

Mi(c)hael Hutchence
Mi(c)hael Ja(c)kson
Mi(c)hael Ma(c)Donald
Mi(c)hael Ma(r)tin Mu(r)phy
Mi(c)hael OB(r)ien
Mi(c)hael Sembello
Mi(c)hael Smith
Mi(c)hael Stipes
Mi(c)hael W. Smith
Mi(c)heal English
Mi(k)e Douglas
Mi(c)key Dolenz
Mi(c)key Rooney
Mi(c)k Glider
Mi(k)e Nesmith
Mi(k)e Ol(d)field
Mi(k)e Reno
Millie Ve(r)on
Mi(r)iam Shaw
Mo(r)gana King
Mo(r)ton Downy
Mu(d)dy Wa(t)ters
Mu(r)iel Lane
My(r)iam He(r)nandez
Nancy Ha(rr)ow
Nancy No(r)man
Nancy Ree(d)
Nancy Yo(r)k
Na(r)vel Felts
Na(t)alie Oreiro
Na(t)alie Cole
Na(t)alie Imbruglia
Na(t)alie Maines
Na(t)alie Me(r)chant
Neal Se(d)aka
Ne(d) Miller
Nelly Fu(r)tado
Ni(c)k Ca(r)ter
Ni(c)k Lachev
Ni(c)olette La(r)son
Nina Go(r)don
No(r)ah Jones
No(r)ma Galli
No(r)man Greenbaum
Os(c)ar De La Ho(y)a
O(t)is Williams
Pa(r)ker Gibbs

Pa((tt)i Austin
Pa(t)ti Dugan
Pa(t)ti Page
Pa(t)ti Smith
Paul Ab(d)ul
Paul An(k)a
Pauline By(r)ne
Paul Ha(r)man
Paul Ma(c)artney
Pea(r)l Bailey
Pe(d)ro Fe(r)nandez
Penny Pa(r)ker
Pe(r)cy Sledge
Pe(r)ry Como
Pe(t)er Cetera
Pe(t)er Frampton
Pe(t)er Gabriel
Pe(t)er To(r)k
Petula Cla(r)k
Pha Te(r)rill
Po(r)ter Wagner
Ra(d)ney Foster
Randy Sc(r)uggs
Ray Cha(r)les
Ray M(c)Kenzie
Ray Pa(r)ker Jr.
Re(d) Ingle
Rex Ha(r)rison
Ri(c)ardo Arjona
Richard Ma(r)x
Ri(c)k Astley
Ri(c)k Sp(r)ingstein
Ri(c)kie Lee Jones
Ri(c)ky Ma(r)tin
Ri(c)ky Nelson
Ri(c) Olasek
Ri(t)a Coolidge
Ri(t)a Hayworth
Ron An(d)erson
Rosco Go(r)don
Rose Ma(r)y Clooney
Ruby Nash Cu(r)tis
Russ Ca(r)lyle
Russ Mo(r)gan
Rusty Goo(d)man
Ruth M(c)Cullough
Ruth Et(t)ing

Sally Ann Ha(r)ris
Sandi Pa(t)ty
Sa(r)ah Br(i)ghtman
Sa(r)ah M(c)Laughlin
Sa(r)ah Vaughan
Scottie Ma(r)sh
Scott M(c)Kenzie
Shannon Ku(r)fman
Shelly Jo(r)don
Shirley Ho(r)n
Solomon Bu(r)ke
Squire Pa(r)sons
Stacy Fe(r)guson
Stan Ri(d)geway
Steve Go(r)me
Steve Pe(r)ry
Steve Wa(r)iner
Steve Wa(r)ner
Steven Cu(r)tis Chapman
Stevie Nic(k)s
Stewart Wa(d)e
Stonewall Ja(c)kson
Sue Do(d)ge
Susan Te(d)eschi
Sussanah M(c)Corkle
Tammy Te(r)rell
Tania Ma(r)ia
Tanya Tu(c)ker
Te(dd)i King
Te(d)dy Grace
Te(d)dy Pendergrass
Te(r)esa Brewer
Te(r)ri De Sa(r)io
Te)r)ry Allen
Te(r)ry Blackwood
Te(r)ry Fei(r)is
Te(r)ry Ja(c)ks
Te(r)ry Shand
Te(r)ry Stafford
The Ju(d)ds
Thelma Ca(r)penter
Tim M(c)Graw
Timmy Yu(r)o
Tina Tu(r)ner
To(d)d Rundgrun
Tom El(d)ridge
Tom Pe(t)ty

Toni Ar(d)en
Tony Ma(r)tin
Tony Sa(c)co
To(r)i Amos
Trace Ad(k)ins
Trey Lo(r)enz
Trisha Yea(r)wood
Twila Pa(r)is
Ty He(r)ndon
Van Mo(r)rison
Ve(r)onique Gens
Vesta Goo(d)man
Vi(c) Damone
Vi(c)ki Ca(r)r
Vi(c)kie Joyce
Vi(c)kie Sue Robinson
Vi(c)ki Spencer
Vi(c)ky Lawrence
Vi)c)tor Ma(r)tin
Vince Ma(r)tell
Vi(r)ginia Hayes
Vi(r)ginia Maxey
Vi(r)ginia Ro(d)riquez
Vi(r)ginia Wynette Pugh
(Tammy Wynette)
Webb Pie(r)ce
Wee Bonny Ba(k)er
Wilbur Ha(r)rison
Wilson Pi(c)kett
Woo(d)y Guthrie
Woo(d)y He(r)man

Other color vocal center people can also be good singers especially when they are double color vocal center people. Any time a person is a double any center color person it has a strong influence on a person operating and cultivating that particular center.

Other Colors
Vocal Center People:

An(n)ette Fu(n)icello - double blue vocal
Ar(n)ie Hai(n)es- double blue vocal
Bi(l)l Ha(l)ey- double yellow vocal
Bi(l)ly Ho(l)liday- double yellow vocal
Bi(l)ly Wi(l)liams- double yellow vocal
Bo(b)by Du(p)rel- double purple vocal
Bo(b)by He(b)b- double purple vocal
Da(l)e Bo(z)zio- double yellow vocal
Da(n) Fo(g)leberg- double blue vocal
Da(n)iel Jo(n)es- double blue vocal
Da(v)id Cr(o)sby- double flesh vocal
De(b)bie Gi(b)son- double purple vocal
De(l)la Ree(s)e- double yellow vocal
Fa(t)s Do(m)ino- double green vocal
Fl(o)yd Cr(a)men- double flesh vocal
Fl(o)yd Kr(a)mer- double flesh vocal
Gi(l)bert O'Su(l)livan- double yellow vocal
Gl(e)n Mi(l)ler- double yellow vocal
Ja(n)is Ia(n)- double blue vocal
Je(f)f Ti(m)mons- double green vocal
Jo(n) Bo(n) Jovi- double blue vocal
Joh(n) De(n)ver- double blue vocal
Joh(n) Fo(g)erty- double blue vocal
Ju(l)io Ig(l)esias- double yellow vocal
Ke(n)dall Pay(n)e- double blue vocal
Lu(c)inda Wi(l)liams- double yellow vocal
Ma(n)fred Ma(n)n- double blue vocal
Me(l) Ti(l)lis- double yellow vocal
Na(n)cy Si(n)atra- double blue vocal
Phi(l) Co(l)lins- double yellow vocal
Phi(l)ip Bai(l)ey- double yellow vocal
Sh(a)nia Tw(a)in- double flesh vocal
St(e)ven Ty(l)er- double yellow vocal
To(n)i Te(n)nille- double blue vocal
To(n)y Be(n)nett- double blue vocal
Wi(l)lie Ne(l)son - double yellow vocal
Fi(n)is He(n)derson- double blue vocal

71

Orange vocal center people also make excellent voice imitators and ventriloquists.

Orange Spectrum - Creativity - Kindness - Versatility
(D, K, R, Y)*   *C's may sound to K   *ia may sound to Y   *tt may sound to D
Orange Vocal Center
Voice Imitators and Ventriloquists

Bob An(d)erson
Geo(r)ge Ki(r)by
Go(r)die Brown
John Roh(r)ke
Rich Li(t)tle
Ron Haw(k)ins
Roy Fi(r)estone

Dan Ho(r)n
David St(r)assman
Edgar Be(r)gen
Ha(rr)y Lester
Ho(r)ace Goldin
Jim Ba(r)ber
Jim Te(t)ar
Richard Po(tt)er
Ron Lu(c)as
Sha(r)i Lewas

YELLOW VOCAL CENTER PEOPLE

Yellow vocal center people are those whose third sounding letters in their first, (middle only if used regularly) or last names are (E), (L), (S) or (Z). For example: Mi(l)ton Ford or Shannon Ke(l)ly. Yellow is the intellectual and analytical color, it is also the positive thinking, cheerful and optimism spectrum. The other positive character attributes of this spectrum are, clarity, comprehension, decisiveness, glorification (of God), logic, and reasonableness. Here are the negative character traits: conniving, deception, pessimism, shrewdness and vindictiveness. Your vocal center colors will stimulate, look and feel conversational, coordinated, harmonious, pleasant, neat, and organized on and around you. Use your vocal center colors in your wardrobe and home-decor to create these images and feelings. The yellow spectrum consists of the light pale yellow's, true hue yellow, gold yellow's and dark copper yellow's. Go to the color fan in the photo section of this book and determine your favorite yellow spectrum colors.

GREEN VOCAL CENTER PEOPLE

Green vocal center people are those whose third sounding letters in their first, middle only if used regularly, or last names are (F), (M), or (T). For example: Sa(m)antha Stewart or Karen Si(m)mons. Green is the spectrum of balance, control (self-control), and peacefulness. The other positive traits of the green spectrum are, caution, cooperativeness, critical, discrimination, equitableness (agreeableness), impartiality (fairness), lawfulness, and poise. The negative traits are, bias, callousness, disagreeableness, envy, lack of judgment, miserliness, sense of injustice and suspicion. Your vocal center colors will stimulate, look, and feel conversational, coordinated, harmonious, pleasant, neat and organized on and around you. Use your vocal center colors in your wardrobe and home-decor to create these images and feelings. The green spectrum ranges from light mint green, true hue green to dark forest green. Go to the color fans in the photo section of this book and determine your favorite green spectrum colors.

BLUE VOCAL CENTER PEOPLE

Blue vocal center people are those whose third sounding letters in their first, middle only if used regularly, or last names are (G), (N), or (U). For example: Ma(g)ie La(n)e or Kevin Jo(n)es. The positive traits of the blue spectrum are: dependability, diplomacy (tactfulness), dutifulness, faithfulness, genius, meditative, open-mindedness, sense of beauty, spacious, and spirited. The negative traits are: apathy, close mindedness, coldness, distrust, indiscretion, lack of faith, lack of spirit, laziness, superstitious, tactlessness and undependability. Your vocal center colors will stimulate look and feel conversational, coordinated, harmonious, pleasant, neat, and organized on and around you. Use your vocal center colors in your wardrobe and home-decor to create these images and feelings. The blue spectrum consists of light baby blues, sky blues, true hue blue, royal blues, navy blues and dark midnight blues. Go to the color fan in the photo section of this book and determine your favorite blue spectrum colors.

Chapter 7

YOUR PHYSICAL CENTER COLORS, TRAIT AND TALENTS

Physical Center
Middle of Chest

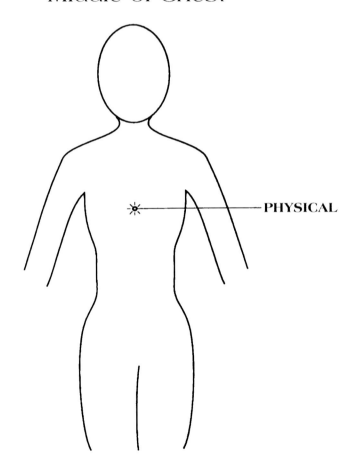

Your physical center is located at the middle of your chest, in the area of your thymus endocrine gland. This is where the eastern philosophies refer to as the heart chakra area. This is the center of our physical abilities, along with being the center in which our compassion, forgiveness, giving, kindness, truthfulness, and warmth originates. We all have heard those old expressions, "The heart never lies", or, "He or she has a giving heart", "Forgive from your heart", or, "That person has a warm, or kind heart". Those that operate and cultivate off of their positive heart center traits project these qualities. Those that cultivate the negative will project the opposite of them. Classic examples of physical/heart center types are: athletes, dancers, philanthropists, runners, weight lifters and those who are just very kind, giving, sincere, truthful, and warm.

In the near future we will be publishing articles, books and producing seminars describing our philosophies on staying in good physical shape, toning muscles, losing weight and our nutritional products line. Just check into our web site www.namecolorology.com and we will keep you posted.

The letters in your names that determine your physical/heart center colors, traits, and talents, are letters that come after the syllable breaks in your first, middle only if used regularly, and your last name. For example: Ru-(b)y Con-(r)ad, this person, looking at the letter-color chart on page 25, you will see is a purple and orange physical/ heart center person. Some people have many syllable breaks in their name therefore having several heart center colors, for example: Al-(a)-(z)an-(d)ra Kan-(d)in-(s)ki. This person would than be a double yellow, single flesh, and double orange physical/ heart center person. Looking at the letter-color chart, determine your physical/heart center colors, then go to the following physical center color sections to find out your specific physical/heart center traits and talents, then go to the color fan in the photo section of this book and determine your favorite physical/heart center spectrum colors. Use dramatic, thick, and warm fabrics and textures in your physical/heart center colors such as corduroys, knits, thick cottons, and wool's. After doing all of the above go to the 3-part chart in the back of the book and record your physical center colors.

To learn the basic steps to cultivate your physical center go to chapter 28.

FLESH PHYSICAL/HEART CENTER PEOPLE

Flesh physical/heart center people are those who have (A), (H), (O), or (V), sounding letters after the syllable breaks in their names. For example: Al-(a)n Baker or Wilma Sil(v)er. The positive or negative character attributes of the flesh spectrum, depending on which ones you cultivate, will be the way in which you project physically, and from your heart. Flesh heart center people are very giving in nature because flesh is the giving color and it is attuned to their giving center. The positive are: articulateness, cleanliness, compensation, coordination, givingness, harmony, introspect, memory recall, morality, organization, practicality, perception, unity (mind-body-soul), and universality. The negative character traits are, confusion, disorderliness, filthiness, forgetfulness, immorality, idolatry, inarticulate, inconsiderateness, inconsistency, lacking coordination, inharmonious, and impracticality. Your physical/heart center colors will look and feel very compassionate, dramatic, forgiving, handsome, kind, physical, sincere, truthful, and warm, on and around you. The flesh spectrum ranges from off whites, beige's, tans, light browns, browns, dark browns and dark chocolate browns. Use your physical/heart center colors in your wardrobe and home-decor to create these images and feelings. Go to the color fan in the photo section of this book and determine your favorite flesh spectrum colors.

PURPLE PHYSICAL/HEART CENTER PEOPLE

Purple physical/heart center people are those who have (B), (I), (P), or (W), sounding letters after syllable breaks in their first, middle only if used regularly, or last names. For example: Re-(b)ecca Anderson or Tina Ho-(b)ert. The positive or negative character attributes of the purple spectrum, depending on which ones you cultivate, will be the way in which you project physically, and from your heart. Purple physical people tend to carry themselves in a dignified, regal, physical manner, since purple is the regal color. The positive traits are: civilized, cultured, dedicated, dignified, empowered, idealistic, intuitive, loyal, mature, regal, self-sacrificing, and tasteful. Their negative traits are, domination, fanaticism, lack of taste, monopolization, pompousness, pettiness, snobbishness, superiority, treachery, uncivilized, and undignified. Your physical/heart center colors will look and feel very compassionate, dramatic, forgiving, handsome, kind, physical, sincere, truthful, and warm, on and around you. The purple spectrum ranges from light lavenders, true hue purple and deep violets. Use your physical/heart center colors in your wardrobe and home-decor to create these images and feelings. Go to the color fan in the photo section of this book and determine your favorite purple spectrum colors.

RED PHYSICAL/HEART CENTER PEOPLE

Red physical/heart center people are those who have (C), (J), (Q), or (X), sounding letters after syllable breaks in their first, middle only if used regularly, or last names. For example: Ra-(c)hel Sanders or Thomas Geor-(g)e (the (g) in this last name phonetically sounds to j). The positive or negative traits of the red spectrum are: beauty of manner (elegance), benevolence (sense of good will), charitableness, chivalry, compassion, courteous (mercifulness), gracefulness, gratefulness (thankfulness), honesty, sincerity, persistence (tenaciousness), physical life energy, valor (courage), and romance. The negative traits of the red spectrum are, brutality, dishonesty, excessive carnal desire, impulsiveness (impatience), jealousy (envy), physical egotism, physical laziness, pitilessness, lack of compassion, rudeness (coarseness), and savageness (barbaric). The traits you will project from your heart will depend on which one's you have cultivated. Your physical/heart center colors will look and feel very compassionate, dramatic, forgiving, handsome, kind, physical, sincere, truthful and warm on and around you. The red spectrum consists of pink reds, rose reds, true hue red, cranberry reds and dark wine reds. Use your physical/heart center colors in your wardrobe and home-decor to create these images and feelings. Go to the color fan in the photo section of this book and determine your favorite red spectrum colors.

ORANGE PHYSICAL/HEART CENTER PEOPLE

Orange physical/heart center people are those who have (D), (K), (R), or (Y), sounding letters after syllable breaks in their first, middle only if used regularly, or last names, for example: San-(d)ra Allison, Re-be-(cc)a Rogers- (the two "c's" in this name, phonetically make the sound of a (k) which is an orange letter, or Bob Bar-(k)er. The positive character traits of the orange spectrum are, affection (fondness), creativity, inspirational enthusiasm, joyfulness, kindness (warm heartedness), repentance, self-assurance, speculation, venturesome, and versatility. The negative traits are, boastfulness, despair (depression), destructiveness, exhibitionism, flamboyance, and unpleasantness. The traits you will project from your heart will depend on which one's you have cultivated. Your physical/heart center colors will look and feel very compassionate, dramatic, forgiving, handsome, kind, physical, sincere, truthful, and warm on and around you. Use your physical/heart center colors in your wardrobe and home-decor to create these images and feelings. The orange spectrum ranges from the light peaches, light corals, true hue orange, rust and dark earthy rust oranges. Go to the color fan in the photo section of this book and determine your favorite orange spectrum colors.

Orange physical/heart center people are very creative physically because of the main character trait of creativity from this spectrum. Look at all of the listed orange physical creative people and how they dominate the following fields.

Orange Spectrum - Creativity - Kindness - Versatility
(D, K, R, Y)*   *C's may sound to K   *ia may sound to Y   *tt may sound to D
Orange Physical Center Baseball Players:

Alex Ro(d)(r)iquez	Chi(ck) Hofy	Fran(k) Howard
An(d)rae Dawson	Chu(ck) Klein	Fran(k)ie Frisch
An(d)res Gala(rr)aga	Cliff Floy(d)	Fran(k) Robinson
An(d)y Van Sly)k)e	Da(rr)ell Evans	Fran(k) Thomas
Ar(k)y Vaughan	Da(rr)ell Strawbe(rr)y	Fre(d) Clar(k)e
Baby Doll Ja(c)obson	Dave Par(k)er	Fre(dd)ie Lindstrom
Barney M(c)(k)os(k)y	De(r)ek Je(t)er	Fre(d) Lynn
Bernie Will(ia)ms	Di(c)k Allen	Fre(d) M(c)Griff
Bibb Fal(k)	Dic(k) Stuart	Fre(d) Will(ia)ms
Bill Dic(k)ey	Du(k)e Sni(d)er	Ga(r)y Car(t)er
Bill Te(rr)y	E(dd)ie Collins	Ga(r)y Gae(tt)i
Billy Will(ia)ms	E(d) Delahan(t)y	Ga(r)y Sheffield
Bobby Boni(ll)a	E(dd)ie Mathews	George Fos(t)er
Bra(d)y An(d)erson	E(dd)ie Mu(rr)y	Ge(r)ald Pe(rr)y
Broo(k)s Robinson	E(dd) Rousch	Greg Luzins(k)i
Cal Rip(k)en	E(d)gar Martinez	Hac(k) Wilson
Can(d)y Mal(d)anal(d)o	Ellis Bur(k)s	Hal Tros(k)y
Carl Yastrzems(k)i	Elmer Fli(ck)	Han(k) Bauer
Carlos Delga(d)o	E(r)ic Davis	Han(k) Greenberg
Carlton Fis(k)	Ernie Ban(k)s	Han(k) Sauer
Cecil Fiel(d)er	Fernan(d)o Vin(a)	Ha(rr)y Heilmann
Charlie Geh(r)inger	Fran(k) Catalano(tt)o	Hen(r)y Han(k) Aa(r)on

Ichi(r)o Suzu(k)i
I(r)ish Meusel
Ivan Ro(d)(r)iquez
Ja(ck) Tobin
Ja(ck) Clar(k)
Ja(ck) Fournier
Ja(ck)ie Robinson
Jeff Bu(rr)oughs
Jeff Ci(r)illio
Je(r)omy Burnitz
Jessee Bur(k)ett
Jimmy O'(R)ou(r)(k)e
Joe A(d)(c)ock
Joe Car(t)er
Joe (D)iMaggio
Joe Jac(k)son
John Ole(r)ud
Jorge Posa(d)a
Jose Canse(c)o
Jose Vi(d)ro
Ken Griffey J(r.)
Ken Will(ia)ms
Kevin M(c)(R)eynolds
Ki(k)i Cuyler
Kirby Pu(c)(k)ett

Lance Pa(rr)ish
La(rr)y Wal(k)er
Lloy(d) Waner
Lou Geh(r)ig
Lu(k)e Appling
Magglio Or(d)onez
Matt Will(ia)ms
Manny Rame(r)iz
Mar(k) Grace
Mar(k) M(c)Gwire
Mic(k)ey Co(c)h(r)ane
Miguel Taja(d)a
Mi(k)e Greenwell
Mi(k)e Piazza
Mi(k)e Schmi(d)t
Mi(k)e Sweeney
Mi(k)e Tiernan
Mic(k)ey Mantle
Orlan(d)o Cepa(d)a
Paul Koner(k)o
Paul La(D)u(c)a
Pe(d)ro Gue(rr)e(r)o
Pete In(c)avialgia
Reggie San(d)ers
Rich Au(r)ila

Ric(k)y Hen(d)erson
Ri(c)o Petrocelli
Rip Ra(d)(c)liff
Rober(t)o Clemen(t)e
Ro(d) Ca(r)ew
Roc(k)ey Colavi(t)o
Roger Ma(r)is
Ron San(t)o
Ruben Sie(rr)a
Rus(t)y Stuab
Spu(d) Davis
Te(d) Kluszens(k)i
Te(d) Will(ia)ms
To(dd) Helton
Tony Pe(r)ez
Tris Spea(k)er
Ty(r)us Cobb
Vla(d)amir Gue(rr)e(r)o
Wa(d)e Boggs
Will(ia)m Clar(k)
Will(ia)m Mc(C)ovey
Will(ia)m Willie Mays
Yoggi Be(rr)a
Za(ck)Wheat

Orange Spectrum - Creativity - Kindness - Versatility
(D, K, R, Y)*   *C's may sound to K   *ia may sound to Y   *tt may sound to D
Orange Physical Center Musicians:

Arthur Dun(c)an
Arthur Mur(r)y
Bud(d)y Rich
Chrissie Hyn(d)e
Di(c)k Kesner
Donald O(c)nnor
E(d)die Van Halen
E(r)ic Clapton
E(r)i(k)a Mo(r)ini
Fre(d) Astaire
Ginger Ro(d)gers

Jer(r)y Lee Lewis
Lars Ul(r)ich
Libe(r)ace
Mi(d)ori
Ni(c)holas Brothers
Pete Star(k)y
Ric(k) Gratton
Ro(d) Morganstein
Ron Wi(k)so
Ter(r)y Bozzio
Vic(t)or Borge--- t sounds to d

Basketball Players

A(d)olph Schayes
A(d)rian Dantley
A(k)eem Olajuwon
An(d)re Miller
An(d)rew Toney
An(d)y Phillips
Antoine Wal)k)er
Bobby M(c)(D)ermott
Bob M(c)A(d)oo
Bob Pe(tt)it
Branch M(c)(k)ra(c)(k)en
By(r)on Scott
Chu(ck) Hyatt
Cly(d)e Drexler
Cly(d)e Frazier
Cly(d)e Lovellette
Connie Haw(k)ins
Ca(r)ol Blazejows(k)i
Di(ck) M(c)guire
Dir(k) Nowitz(k)i
Do(c)(t)or Julius Erving
Domin(q)ue Wil(k)ins
Earl Mon(r)oe
E(dd)y Jones
E(d) Krause
E(d) Ma(c)auley
El(d)en Campbell
El(t)on Bran(d)
E(r)ic Floy(d)
Fran(k) V. Ramsey
Gail Goo(d)(r)ich
Ga(r)y Payton

George Mi(k)an
Han(k) Luisetti
Ha(r)old Bu(d) Fos(t)er
Ha(r)old Hal Greer
Ha(rr)y Bu(dd)y Jeannette
Ha(rr)y Gallatin
Hen(r)y Denhart
Ja(ck) M(c)(C)ra(k)en
Ja(ck) Si(k)ma
Ja(ck) Twyman
Jason Ki(dd)
Je(rr)y Lu(c)as
Je(rr)y Stac(k)house
Je(rr)y West
Joe Ful(k)s
John Hon(d)o Havlicec(k)
John Sto(ck)(t)on
John Woo(d)en
Ka(r)eem Ab(d)ul Jabbar
Kevin M(c)Hale
Ki(k)i Van(d)eweghe
La(rr)y Bir(d)
La(rr)y Hughes
Lau(r)en La(dd)ie Gale
Lenny Wil(k)ins
Mar(k) Agui(rr)e
Mar(k) Jac(k)son
Mar(q)ues Haynes
Mar(q)ues Johnson
Mau(r)ice Chee(k)s
Mi(c)hael Cooper
Mi(c)hael Jor(d)an

Mi(k)e Bibby
Ne(r)a D. White
Ni(ck) Van Exel
Orlan(d)o Woolridge
Os(c)ar Robertson
Paul J A(r)izin
Pre(d)(r)aq Stoja(k)ovic
Ric(k) Ba(rr)y
Robert Fuzzy Van(d)ivier
Sha(r)eef Ab(d)ur Rahim
Shawn Ma(r)ion
Si(d)ney Mon(c)rief
Sla(t)er Martin
Te(rr)y Cummings
Tim Dun(c)an
Tim Har(d)away
Tracy M(c)Gra(d)y
Vern Mi(kk)elsen
Vin Ba(k)er
Vince Car(t)er
Wayman Tils(d)ale
Will(ia)m Bill Bra(d)ley
Will(ia)m Bill Russell
Will(ia)m Bill Sharman
Will(ia)m Bill Walton
Will(ia)m Billy Cunningham
Will(ia)m Johnson
Will(ia)m Pop Gates
Willis Ree(d)
Xavier M(c)(d)aniels

Auguste Ro(d)in
Giovanni Lo(r)enzo Bernini
Mi(c)helangelo Buona(r)ro(t)i
San(t)i Rapheal
Isa(d)ora Dun(c)an--dancer

YELLOW PHYSICAL/HEART CENTER PEOPLE

Yellow physical/heart center people are those who have (E), (L), (S), or (Z), sounding letters after syllable breaks in their first, middle only if used regularly, or last names. For example: Al-(l)i-(s)on Randall, this person is a double yellow physical/heart center person, or Megan Ash-(l)ey. Yellow is the intellectual and analytical color. It is also the positive thinking, cheerful, and optimistic spectrum. The other positive character attributes of this spectrum are, clarity, comprehension, decisiveness, glorification (of God), logic, and reasonableness. Here are the negative character traits: conniving, deception, pessimism, shrewdness and vindictiveness. Your physical/heart center colors will look and feel very compassionate, dramatic, forgiving, handsome, kind, physical, sincere, truthful, and warm, on and around you. The yellow spectrum consists of the light pale yellow's, true hue yellow, gold yellow's, and dark copper yellow's. Use your physical/heart center colors in your wardrobe and home-decor to create these images and feelings. Go to the color fan in the photo section of this book and determine your favorite yellow spectrum colors.

GREEN PHYSICAL/HEART CENTER PEOPLE

Green physical/heart center people are those who have (F), (M), or (T), sounding letters after syllable breaks in their first, middle only if used regularly, or last names. For example: A-(m)anda Sellers or Julie Wes-(m)in-is-(t)er. Green is the spectrum of balance, control (self-control), and peacefulness. The other positive traits of the green spectrum are, caution, cooperativeness, critical, discrimination, equitableness (agreeableness), impartiality (fairness), lawfulness, and poise. The negative traits are: bias, callousness, disagreeableness, envy, lack of judgment, miserliness, sense of injustice and suspicion. (Note: green heart center people must guard against being to callous and unfeeling physically and from their heart, because of the "callousness" character trait of this spectrum.) Instead, cultivate the peaceful, agreeableness and understanding traits of this spectrum. Your physical/heart center colors will look and feel very compassionate, dramatic, forgiving, handsome, kind, physical, sincere, truthful, and warm, on and around you. Use your physical/heart center colors in your wardrobe and home-decor to create these images and feelings. The green spectrum ranges from light mint green, true hue green to dark forest green. Go to the color fan in the photo section of this book and determine your favorite green spectrum colors.

BLUE PHYSICAL/HEART CENTER PEOPLE

Blue physical/heart center people are those who have (G), (N), or (U), sounding letters after syllable breaks in their first, middle only if used regularly, or last names. For example: Na-(n)ette Carson or Brenda Gre-(g)ory. The positive traits of the blue spectrum are: dependability, diplomacy (tactfulness), dutifulness, faithfulness, genius, meditative, open-mindedness, sense of beauty, spacious and spirited. The negative traits they need to guard against are: apathy, close mindedness, coldness, distrust, indiscretion, lack of faith, lack of spirit, laziness, superstitious, tactlessness, and undependability. Your physical/heart center colors will look and feel very compassionate, dramatic, forgiving, handsome, kind, physical, sincere, truthful, and warm, on and around you. The blue spectrum consists of light baby blues, sky blues, true hue blue, royal blues, navy blues and dark midnight blues. Use your physical/heart center colors in your wardrobe and home-decor to create these images and feelings. Go to the color fan in the photo section of this book and determine your favorite blue spectrum colors.

Chapter 8

YOUR CONTROL CENTER COLORS, TRAITS AND TALENTS

Control Center
Upper Solar Plexis

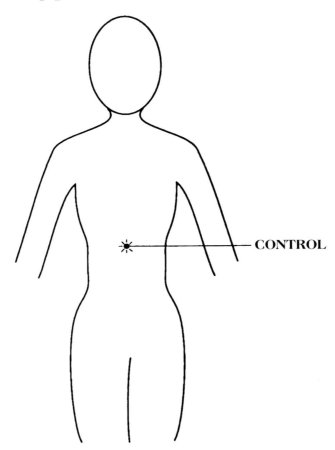

Your control center is located in the solar plexus area of your body in between your lower ribs, in the area of your adrenal endocrine gland, and the area eastern philosophies call the solar plexus chakra center. This is the center in which our abilities to control our emotions, feelings, impulses and negative habits and addictions originates along with being the center which we derive our self-esteem, dignity, and self empowerment. This is our, "flight or fight" center. I also call this center the corporate/business center. This is the center that tells you the colors you want to wear to command higher wages or job positions and get more respect. Those that cultivate and operate off of their positive traits of this center are those who always seem to be dignified, empowered, formal, business like, in control and command a lot of respect. Classic examples of the control center type are: antique dealers, ballet dancers, classical musicians, corporate business men and women, cultural art historians, diplomats, formal instructors, glamorous models, nobility, and certain athletes, such as professional bowlers, divers, pool players, posture and image instructors, relief pitchers and quarterbacks.

The letters in your name that determine your control center colors, traits, and talents are the letters before any of the syllable brakes in your name. For example: J(u)-lie A(n)-de(r)-son, looking at the color- letter chart on page 25, you would see this name person is a double blue and orange color control/center person. Looking at the letter-color chart determine your control center colors then go to the following control center color sections to find out your specific control center traits and talents, then go to the color fan in the photo section of this book and determine your favorite control center spectrum colors. Use your control center colors in very dignified, formal, refined, rich, and tailored prints and materials such as: gabardines, silks, and smooth light weight wool's. After doing all of the above go to the 3-part chart in the back of the book and record your control center colors.

To learn the basic steps to cultivate your control center go to chapter 28.

FLESH SPECTRUM CONTROL CENTER PEOPLE

Flesh spectrum control center people are those who's letters before the syllable breaks in their first, middle only if used regularly, and last names are (A), (H), (0) or (V) letters. For example: (A)-dam Willis, Sandy L(a)-ton or (A)my li(v)-ingston. The positive or negative character attributes of the flesh spectrum, depending on which ones you cultivate, will be the way in which you project from your control center. The positive are: articulateness, cleanliness, compensation, coordination, giving-ness, harmony, introspective, memory recall, morality, organization, practicality, perception, unity (mind-body-soul), and universality. The negative character traits are, confusion, disorderliness, filthiness, forgetfulness, immorality, idolatry, inarticulate, inconsiderateness, inconsistency, lacking coordination, inharmonious, and impractical. Your control center colors will look and feel very business like, dignified, empowered, formal, and in-control on and around you. The flesh spectrum ranges from off whites, beige's, tans, light browns, browns, dark browns and dark chocolate browns. Use your control center colors in your wardrobe and home-decor to create these images and feelings. Go to the color fan in the photo section of this book and determine your favorite flesh spectrum colors.

PURPLE SPECTRUM CONTROL CENTER PEOPLE

Purple spectrum control center people are those whose letters before the syllable breaks in their first, middle only if used regularly, and last names are (B), (I), (P) or (W). For example: (I)-leen Randall or M(i)-cheal Anderson. The positive or negative character attributes of the purple spectrum, depending on which ones you cultivate, will be the way in which you project from your control center. The positive are: civilized, cultured, dedicated, dignified, empowered, idealistic, intuitive, loyal, mature, regal, self-sacrificing and tasteful. The negative traits are: domination, fanaticism, lack of taste, monopolization, pompousness, pettiness, snobbishness, superiority, treachery, uncivilized, and undignified. Your control center colors will look, and feel, very business like, dignified, empowered, formal, and in control, on and around you. The purple spectrum ranges from light lavenders, true hue purple and deep violets. Use your control center colors in your wardrobe and home-decor to create these images and feelings. Go to the color fan in the photo section of this book and determine your favorite purple spectrum colors.

RED SPECTRUM CONTROL CENTER PEOPLE

Red spectrum control center people are those whose letters before the syllable breaks in their first, middle only if used regularly, or last names are (C), (J), (Q) or (X). For example: (X)-avier Roland or Roberta Ale(x)-us. The positive traits of the red spectrum, depending on which one's you have cultivated, are: beauty of manner (elegance), benevolence (sense of good will), charitableness, chivalry, compassion, courteous (mercifulness), gracefulness, gratefulness (thankfulness), honesty (sincerity), persistence (tenaciousness), physical life energy, romance, and valor (courage). The negative traits of the red spectrum are: brutality, dishonesty, excessive carnal desire, impulsiveness (impatience), jealousy (envy), physical egotism, physical laziness, pitilessness (lack of compassion), rudeness (coarseness), savageness (barbaric). Your control center colors will look and feel very business like, dignified, empowered, formal, and in-control, on and around you. The red spectrum consists of pink reds, rose reds, true hue red, cranberry reds and dark wine reds. Use your control center colors in your wardrobe and home-decor to create these images and feelings. Go to the color fan in the photo section of this book and determine your favorite red spectrum colors.

ORANGE SPECTRUM CONTROL CENTER PEOPLE

Orange spectrum control center people are those whose letters before the syllable breaks in their first, middle only if used regularly, or last names are (D), (K), (R) or (Y). For example: Ca(r)-ol Riley or Robin Pe-te(r)-son. The positive traits of the orange spectrum, depending on which one's you have cultivated, are, affection (fondness), creativity, inspirational enthusiasm, joyfulness, kindness (warm heartedness), repentance, self-assurance, speculation, venturesome, versatility. The negative traits are, boastfulness, despair (depression), destructiveness, exhibitionism, flamboyance, and unpleasantness. The traits you will project from your control center will depend on which one's you have cultivated. Your control center colors will look and feel very business like, dignified, empowered, formal, and in-control, on and around you. The orange spectrum ranges from the light peaches, light corals, true hue orange, rust and dark earthy rust oranges. Use your control center colors in your wardrobe and home-decor to create these images and feelings. Go to the color fan in the photo section of this book and determine your favorite orange spectrum colors.

YELLOW SPECTRUM CONTROL CENTER PEOPLE

Yellow control center people are those whose letters, before the syllable breaks in their first, middle only if used regularly, or last names are: (E), (L), (S), or (Z). For example: Ke(ll)-y Roberts or Angie Le(s)-lie. Yellow is the intellectual and analytical color. It is also the positive thinking, cheerful, and optimism spectrum. The other positive character attributes of this spectrum are, clarity, comprehension, decisiveness, glorification (of God), logic, and reasonableness. Here are the negative character traits: conniving, deception, pessimism, shrewdness and vindictiveness. These are the traits you will project from your control center depending on which one's you have cultivated. Your control center colors will look and feel very business like, dignified, empowered, formal, and in-control, on and around you. The yellow spectrum ranges from the light pale yellow's, true hue yellow, gold yellow's and dark copper yellow's. Use your control center colors in your wardrobe and home-decor to create these images and feelings. Go to the color fan in the photo section of this book and determine your favorite yellow spectrum colors.

GREEN SPECTRUM CONTROL CENTER PEOPLE

Green control center people are those whose letters before the syllable breaks in their first, middle only if used regularly, or last names are: (F), (M), or (T). For example: Ta(m)-my Lipsky or Dorothy Sa(m)-uel. Green is the spectrum of balance, control (self-control), and peacefulness. The other positive traits of the green spectrum are, caution, cooperation, critical, discrimination, equitableness (agreeableness), impartiality (fairness), lawfulness, and poise. The negative traits are: bias, callousness, disagreeableness, envy, lack of judgment, miserliness, sense of injustice, and suspicion. Your control center colors will look and feel very business like, dignified, empowered, formal, and in control, on and around you. The green spectrum ranges from light mint green, true hue green to dark forest green. Use your control center colors in your wardrobe and home-decor to create these images and feelings. Go to the color fan in the photo section of this book and determine your favorite green spectrum colors.

BLUE SPECTRUM CONTROL CENTER PEOPLE

Blue control center people are those whose letters before the syllable breaks in their first, middle only if used regularly, or last names are: (G), (N), or (U). For example: Da(n)-iel Pickerson or Paula S(u)san. The positive traits of the blue spectrum are: dependability, diplomacy (tactfulness), dutifulness, faithfulness, genius, meditative, open-mindedness, sense of beauty, spacious, and spirited. The negative traits they need to guard against are: apathy, close mindedness, coldness, distrust, indiscretion, lack of faith, lack of spirit, laziness, superstition, tactlessness, and undependability. Your control center colors will look and feel very business like, dignified, empowered, formal, and in-control, on and around you. The blue spectrum consists of light baby blues, sky blues, true hue blue, royal blues, navy blues and dark midnight blues. Use your control center colors in your wardrobe and home-decor to create these images and feelings. Go to the color fan in the photo section of this book and determine your favorite blue spectrum colors.

Chapter 9

YOUR EMOTIONAL/ROMANTIC CENTER COLORS,
TRAITS AND TALENTS

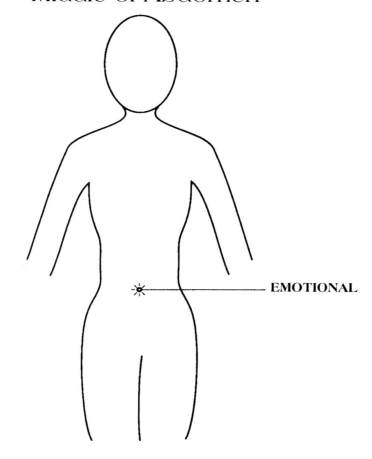

Emotional Center
Middle of Abdomen

EMOTIONAL

Your emotional/romantic center is located at your navel in the general area of your pancreas endocrine gland and the area the eastern philosophies call the navel chakra. This is the center in which our emotional and romantic soulful feelings come from. I also call it the soul, relax, and contentment center, because until a person finds a true soulful romantic mate they will never completely be relaxed and content. "Satisfying the soul" is what we all strive for, and we have all heard the expression that, "love cures all". I also call this center the feminine center, for different reasons. First, because women are very emotional and romantic by nature (just look at who buys the vast majority of romantic novels, clothing, gifts etc.), along with the fact that this is the area in which women have their womb. 70% or more of women pick their emotional center colors along with their spiritual center colors as their favorites. Classic examples of those that cultivate and operate off of this center are, romantic apparel designers, romantic writers, and those that always seem to be very feminine, soft, relaxed, romantic or content. There are new theories now that say, emotional intelligence, is possibly more important to a person becoming successful then their, IQ intelligence. I believe that a person's emotional intelligence should be cultivated, but I also believe that their emotional intelligence is a reflection of their spiritual moral center maturity, and also their common sense intellectual center maturity along with their other centers maturity. It simply is a combination of many of your centers maturity. How can you analyze a person without looking at all their center's personalities? Many people in the world base success just on financial status when really we know there are other different forms of success. The letters that determine your emotional/romantic center colors are the letters that you "do not have" in your names for example: "Sandra Piper". As you can see by looking at the letter-color chart on page 25 this name has two yellow letters, two flesh, one blue, three orange and three purple. This name has no red color letters of C, J, Q or X and no green letters of F, M, or T, so the colors in the red and green spectrums would be this person's emotional colors. Note: if you have all seven of the letter colors in your name, such as (Nancy Waterfield), then your emotional colors will be in the neutral gray spectrum. If you happen to be a gray emotional person just read the character traits of the gray spectrum listed in chapter 2 and those will be the traits you project emotionally. Looking at the letter-color chart, determine your emotional center colors, then go to the following emotional center color sections to find out your specific emotional center traits and talents, then go to the color fan in the photo section of this book and determine your favorite emotional center spectrum colors. Use your emotional/romantic colors in fabrics that are flowing, passive, soft, relaxed, and romantic, textures and prints. After doing all of the above go to the 3-part chart in the back of the book and record your emotional center colors. To learn how to cultivate your emotional center go to chapter 28.

FLESH SPECTRUM EMOTIONAL/ROMANTIC CENTER PEOPLE

Flesh spectrum emotional/romantic center people are those that have no flesh spectrum color sounding letters of (A), (H), (O), or (V) in their names, for example: Jill Kiley or Mike Green. The positive or negative character attributes of the flesh spectrum, depending on which ones you cultivate, will be the way in which you project from your emotional center. The positive are: articulateness, cleanliness, compensation, coordination, giving ness, harmony, introspect, memory recall, morality, organization, practicality, perception, unity (mind-body-soul), and universality. The negative character traits are: confusion, disorderliness, filthiness, forgetfulness, immorality, idolatry, inarticulate, inconsiderateness, inconsistency, lacking coordination, inharmonious, and impracticality. Your emotional center colors will look and feel very content, emotional, passive, peaceful, relaxed, soft, soulful and romantic, on and around you. The flesh spectrum ranges from off whites, beige's, tans, light browns, browns, dark browns and dark chocolate browns. Use your emotional center colors to create these moods and feelings in your home-decor and wardrobe. Go to the color fan in the photo section of this book and determine your favorite flesh spectrum colors.

PURPLE EMOTIONAL/ROMANTIC CENTER PEOPLE

Purple spectrum emotional/romantic center people are those that have no purple spectrum color sounding letters of (B), (I), (P), or (W), in their names, for example: Sally Kramer or Jenny Alcott. The positive or negative character attributes of the purple spectrum, depending on which ones you cultivate, will be the way in which you project from your emotional center, the positive are: civilized, cultured, dedicated, dignified, empowered, idealistic, intuitive, loyal, mature, regal, self sacrificing, and tasteful. The negative traits are, domination, fanaticism, lack of taste, monopolization, pompousness, pettiness, snobbishness, superiority, treachery, uncivilized, and undignified. Your emotional center colors will look and feel very content, emotional, passive, peaceful, relaxed, soft, and romantic on and around you. The purple spectrum ranges from light lavenders, true hue purple and deep violets. Use your emotional center colors in your wardrobe and home-decor to create these images and feelings. Go to the color fan in the photo section of this book and determine your favorite purple spectrum colors.

RED EMOTIONAL/ROMANTIC CENTER PEOPLE

Red spectrum emotional/romantic center people are those that have no red spectrum color sounding letters of (C), (J), (Q), or (X) in their names. For example: Mike Ronalds or Cathy Miller, (the C in Cathy phonetically sounds to K so it is not considered a red letter but an orange letter). The positive or negative traits of the red spectrum, depending on which one's you have cultivated, the positive are, beauty of manner (elegance), benevolence (sense of good will), charitableness, chivalry, compassion, courteous (mercifulness), gracefulness, gratefulness (thankfulness), honesty (sincerity), persistence (tenaciousness), physical life energy, romance, and valor (courage). The negative traits of the red spectrum are: brutality, dishonesty, excessive carnal desire, impulsiveness (impatience), jealousy (envy), physical egotism, physical laziness, pitilessness (lack of compassion), rudeness (coarseness), savageness (barbaric). Your emotional center colors will look and feel very content, passive, peaceful, relaxed, romantic, soft, and soulful on and around you. The red spectrum consists of pink reds, rose reds, true hue red, cranberry reds and dark wine reds. Use your emotional center colors in your wardrobe and home-decor to create these images and feelings. Go to the color fan in the photo section of this book and determine your favorite red spectrum colors.

ORANGE EMOTIONAL/ROMANTIC CENTER PEOPLE

Orange spectrum emotional/romantic center people are those that have no orange spectrum color sounding letters of (D), (K), (R), or (Y), in their names. For example: Jim Sully or Beth Smith. The positive or negative traits of the orange spectrum, depending on which one's you have cultivated, are: affection (fondness), creativity, inspirational enthusiasm, joyfulness, kindness (warm heartedness), repentance, self-assurance, speculation, venturesome, and versatility. The negative traits are, boastfulness, despair (depression), destructiveness, exhibitionism, flamboyance and unpleasantness. Your emotional center colors will look and feel very content, passive, peaceful, relaxed, romantic, soft, and soulful on and around you. Use your emotional center colors in your wardrobe and home-decor to create these images and feelings. The orange spectrum ranges from the light peaches, light corals, true hue orange, rust and dark earthy rust oranges. Go to the color fan in the photo section of this book and determine your favorite orange spectrum colors.

YELLOW EMOTIONAL/ROMANTIC CENTER PEOPLE

Yellow spectrum emotional/romantic center people are those that have no yellow spectrum color sounding letters of (E), (L), (S), or (Z), in their names. For example: Pam Young or Tom Mann. Yellow is the intellectual and analytical color. It is also the positive thinking, cheerful, and optimistic spectrum. The other positive character attributes of this spectrum are, clarity, comprehension, decisiveness, glorification (of God), logic, and reasonability. The negative character traits: conniving, deception, pessimism, shrewdness, and vindictiveness. These are the traits you will project from your emotional center depending on which one's you have cultivated. Your emotional center colors will look and feel very content, passive, peaceful, relaxed, romantic, soft, and soulful on and around you. The yellow spectrum ranges from the light pale yellow's, true hue yellow, gold yellow's and dark copper yellow's. Use your emotional center colors in your wardrobe and home-decor to create these images and feelings. Go to the color fan in the photo section of this book and determine your favorite yellow spectrum colors.

GREEN EMOTIONAL/ROMANTIC CENTER PEOPLE

Green spectrum emotional/romantic center people are those that have no green spectrum color sounding letters of (F), (M), or (T), in their names. For example: Elisa Parkinson or Lillian Page. Green is the spectrum of balance, control (self-control), and peacefulness. The other positive traits of the green spectrum are, caution, cooperation, critical, discrimination, equitableness (agreeableness), impartiality (fairness), lawfulness, and poise. The negative traits are: bias, callousness, disagreeableness, envy, lack of judgment, miserliness, sense of injustice, and suspicion. Your emotional center colors will look and feel very content, passive, peaceful, relaxed, romantic, soft, and soulful on and around you. The green spectrum ranges from light mint green, true hue green to dark forest green. Use your emotional center colors in your wardrobe and home-decor to create these images and feelings. Go to the color fan in the photo section of this book and determine your favorite green spectrum colors.

BLUE EMOTIONAL/ROMANTIC CENTER PEOPLE

Blue spectrum emotional/romantic center people are those that have no blue spectrum color sounding letters of (G), (N), or (U), in their names. For example: Harold Boyd or Sarah Potter.

The positive traits of the blue spectrum are: dependability, diplomacy (tactfulness), dutifulness, faithfulness, genius, meditative, open-mindedness, sense of beauty, spacious, and spirited. The negative traits they need to guard against are: apathy, close mindedness, coldness, distrust, indiscretion, lack of faith, lack of spirit, laziness, superstitious, tactlessness, and undependability. Your emotional center colors will look and feel very content, passive, peaceful, relaxed, romantic, soft, and soulful on and around you. The blue spectrum consists of light baby blues, sky blues, true hue blue, royal blues, navy blues and dark midnight blues. Use your emotional center colors in your wardrobe and home-decor to create these images and feelings. Go to the color fan in the photo section of this book and determine your favorite blue spectrum colors.

Chapter 10

YOUR SEXUAL CENTER COLORS, TRAITS, AND TALENTS

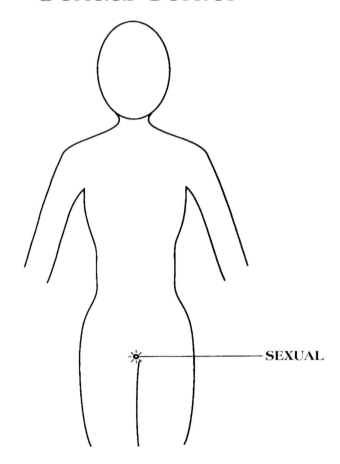

Sexual Center

SEXUAL

Your sexual center is located in the lower middle pelvis area, the eastern philosophies call this the root chakra center. For women it is in the area of their ovary endocrine gland, for men it is the testes endocrine gland area. Your sexual center has five main functions: reproduction, sexual pleasure, eliminating waste and toxins, along with being your survival and grounding center. The reason for calling it the survival and grounding center is because this is the center in which we are forced to rely on making critical decisions in certain circumstances when we need to ground ourselves to survive hard or serious situations. For example: if a person finds themselves financially broke without a job with the rent to pay and mouths to feed, they must "ground" themselves first and say, "What do I have to do to survive this critical situation"? Classic examples of those that cultivate and operate off of this center are glamorous movie stars, (Carry Grant, Mae West, Marliyn Monroe etc.) professional models, and professional dancers. Sexual center types act, talk, walk and project sexy.

The letters in your name that determines your sexual center colors are the last sounding letters in your first, middle only if used regularly, and last names. For example: Juli(e) Jackso(n). Looking at the color-letter chart on page 25 You will see this name example person is a yellow and blue sexual center person. Another example: Wal(t) Ale(x) this person is a green and red sexual center person. Look at the letter-color chart to determine your sexual center colors, then go to the following sexual center color sections to find out your specific sexual center traits and talents. Now go to the color fan in the photo section of this book and determine your favorite sexual center spectrum colors. Use your sexual center colors in fabrics that are alluring, glamorous, seductive, secretive, sexy, sheer, shimmering, suave, or earthy. After doing all of the above go to the 3-part chart in the back of the book and record your sexual center colors. To learn how to cultivate your sexual center go to chapter 28.

FLESH SPECTRUM SEXUAL CENTER PEOPLE

Flesh spectrum sexual center people are those whose last sounding letters in their first, middle only if used regularly, or last name end in a flesh sounding letter of (A), (H), (O) or (V). For example: Lind(a) Scates or Shan(a) Sacc(a), this name example is a double flesh sexual center person. The positive or negative character attributes of the flesh spectrum, depending on which ones you cultivate, will be the way in which you project from your sexual center. The positive are: articulateness, cleanliness, compensation, coordination, giving ness, harmony, introspect, memory recall, morality, organization, practicality, perception, unity (mind-body-soul), and universality. The negative character traits are: confusion, disorderliness, filthiness, forgetfulness, immorality, idolatry, inarticulateness, inconsiderateness, inconsistency, lacking coordination, inharmonious, and impracticality. Your sexual center colors will look and feel very glamorous, seductive, secretive, sexy, sheer, suave, or earthy on and around you. The flesh spectrum ranges from off whites, beige's, tans, light browns, browns, dark browns and dark chocolate browns. Use your sexual center colors to create these feelings in your home-decor and wardrobe. Go to the color fan in the photo section of this book and determine your favorite flesh spectrum colors.

PURPLE SPECTRUM SEXUAL CENTER PEOPLE

Purple spectrum sexual center people are those whose last sounding letters in their first, middle only if used regularly, or last name end in a purple sounding letter of (B), (I), (P), or (W). For example: Bo(b) Roberts or Sandy Philli(p)The positive or negative character attributes of the purple spectrum, depending on which ones you cultivate will be the way in which you project from your sexual center. The positive attributes are: civilized, cultured, dedicated, dignified, empowered, idealistic, intuitive, loyal, mature, regal, self-sacrificing and tasteful. The negative traits are, domination, fanaticism, lack of taste, monopolization, pompousness, pettiness, snobbishness, superiority, treachery, uncivilized, and undignified. Your sexual center colors will look and feel very glamorous, seductive, secretive, sexy, sheer, suave, or earthy, on and around you. The purple spectrum ranges from light lavenders, true hue purple and deep violets. Use your sexual center colors in your wardrobe and home-decor to create these images and feelings. Go to the color fan in the photo section of this book and determine your favorite purple spectrum colors.

RED SPECTRUM SEXUAL CENTER PEOPLE

Red spectrum sexual center people are those whose last sounding letters in their first, middle only if used regularly, or last name end in a red sounding letter of (C), (J), (Q), or (X), for example: Sta(c)y Walker, the (y) in this name is silent so this name phonetically sounds to Sta-(c), or Barbara Re(x).The positive traits of the red spectrum, depending on which one's you have cultivated, are: beauty of manner (elegance), benevolence (sense of good will), charitableness, chivalry, compassion, courteous (mercifulness), gracefulness, gratefulness (thankfulness), honesty (sincerity), persistence (tenaciousness), physical life energy, valor (courage), and romance. The negative traits of the red spectrum are: brutality, dishonesty, excessive carnal desire, impulsiveness (impatience), jealousy (envy), physical egotism, physical laziness, pitilessness (lack of compassion), rudeness (coarseness), and savageness (barbaric). Your sexual center colors will look and feel very glamorous, seductive, secretive, sexy, sheer, suave, or earthy, on and around you. The red spectrum consists of pink reds, rose reds, true hue red, cranberry reds and dark wine reds. Use your sexual center colors in your wardrobe and home-decor to create these images and feelings. Go to the color fan in the photo section of this book and determine your favorite red spectrum colors.

ORANGE SPECTRUM SEXUAL CENTER PEOPLE

Orange spectrum sexual center people are those whose last sounding letters in their first, middle only if used regularly, or last name end in a orange sounding letter of (D), (K), (R) or (Y), for example: Mac(k) Stewart or Jane Mille(r). The positive traits of the orange spectrum, depending on which one's you have cultivated, are: affection (fondness), creativity, inspirational enthusiasm, joyfulness, kindness (warm heartedness), repentance, self-assurance, speculation, venturesome, and versatility. The negative traits are, boastfulness, despair (depression), destructiveness, exhibitionism, flamboyance and unpleasantness. Your sexual center colors will look and feel very glamorous, seductive, secretive, sexy, sheer, suave, or earthy, on and around you. The orange spectrum ranges from the light peaches, light corals, true hue orange, rust and dark earthy rust oranges. Use your sexual center colors to create these feelings in your home-decor and wardrobe. Go to the color fan in the photo section of this book and determine your favorite orange spectrum colors.

YELLOW SPECTRUM SEXUAL CENTER PEOPLE

Yellow spectrum sexual center people are those whose last sounding letters in their first, middle only if used regularly, or last name end in a yellow sounding letter of (E), (L), (S) or (Z), for example: Nelli(e) Norten or Karen Mill(s). Yellow is the intellectual and analytical color. It is also the positive thinking, cheerful, and optimistic spectrum, the other positive traits of the yellow spectrum, depending on which one's you have cultivated, are: clarity, comprehension, decisiveness, glorification (of God), logic, and reasonableness. The negative character traits: conniving, deception, pessimism, shrewdness, and vindictiveness. Your sexual center colors will look and feel very glamorous, seductive, secretive, sexy, sheer, suave, or earthy, on and around you. The yellow spectrum ranges from the light pale yellow's, true hue yellow, gold yellow's and dark copper yellow's. Use your sexual center colors to create these feelings in your home-decor and wardrobe. Go to the color fan in the photo section of this book and determine your favorite yellow spectrum colors.

GREEN SPECTRUM SEXUAL CENTER PEOPLE

Green spectrum sexual center people are those whose last sounding letters in their first, middle only if used regularly, or last name end in a green sounding letter of (F), (M), or (T), for example: Jennifer Alcu(tt) or Ma(tt) Barren. The positive traits of the green spectrum are, caution, cooperation, critical, discrimination, equitableness (agreeableness), impartiality (fairness), lawfulness, and poise. The negative traits are: bias, callousness, disagreeableness, envy, lack of judgment, miserliness, sense of injustice, and suspicion. Your sexual center colors will look and feel very glamorous, seductive, secretive, sexy, sheer, suave, or earthy, on and around you. The green spectrum ranges from light mint green, true hue green to dark forest green. Use your sexual center colors to create these feelings in your home-decor and wardrobe. Go to the color fan in the photo section of this book and determine your favorite green spectrum colors.

BLUE SPECTRUM SEXUAL CENTER PEOPLE

Blue spectrum sexual center people are those whose last sounding letters in their first, middle only if used regularly, or last name end in a blue sounding letter of (G), (N), or (U). For example: Gre(g) Sutter or Paula Elle(n). The positive traits of the blue spectrum are: dependability, diplomacy (tactfulness), dutifulness, faithfulness, genius, meditative, open-mindedness, sense of beauty, spacious, and spirited. The negative traits they need to guard against are: apathy, close mindedness, coldness, distrust, indiscretion, lack of faith, lack of spirit, laziness, superstitious, tactlessness, and undependability. Your sexual center colors will look and feel very glamorous, seductive, secretive, sexy, sheer, suave, or earthy, on and around you. The blue spectrum consists of light baby blues, sky blues, true hue blue, royal blues, navy blues and dark midnight blues. Use your sexual center colors to create these feelings in your home-decor and wardrobe. Go to the color fan in the photo section of this book and determine your favorite blue spectrum colors.

Chapter 11

MODEL PHOTOGRAPHS AND YOUR COLOR FANS

ALL INQUIRIES ABOUT THE MODELS USED IN THIS BOOK OR OTHER
NAME COLOROLOGY MEDIA PHOTOGRAPHS SHOULD CONTACT US
AT www.namecolorology.com OR CALL 1-877-505-9100

Emma Guglielmana
Emotional/Romantic Center Color
Feminine-Romantic-Soulful

98

Jill Smith
Emotional/Romantic Center Color
Emotional-Romantic-Soulful

109

Ki(m) William(s)
Glamorous/Sexual Center Colors
Alluring-Glamorous-Sexy
110

K(i)m W(i)lliams
Mental/Intellectual Center Colors
Intellectual-Logical-Practical

111

(C)helsea Davis
Spiritual/Wholesome Center Color
Happy-Spirited-Youthful

Ev(a) Gholson
Sexual/Glamorous Center Color
Alluring-Glamorous-Sexy

119

flesh	purples	purples	purples	reds	reds	reds	oranges	oranges	oranges
○	○	○	○	○	○	○	○	○	○

yellows	yellows	yellows	greens	greens	greens	blues	blues	blues	neutrals
○	○	○	○	○	○	○	○	○	○

123

Chapter 12

SHOPPING FOR AND BUILDING A WARDROBE USING YOUR CENTER/COLORS

The first step in shopping for your different center/color image garments is first to determine which center type outfits you need the most. Is it your control/corporate business, emotional/romantic, or your glamorous sexy center outfit? Once you have decided which one you want to project, I have found the best results to acquiring these garments, is to shop for your desired colors, prints, textures and styles at fabric stores. It has been my personal experience, shopping for my models and others, that I am able to find these materials in the first or second fabric stores that I go to close to 70% of the time. Where in other cases when I try to find the colors and styles I am looking for in fashion stores it has been very hard to find them the majority of the time. You will also find out shopping in the fabric stores that you will not only find what your looking for easier, but you will have a greater variety of positive choices. The fabric sales people will almost always be able to help you find what your looking for, plus they can tell you how many yards of material you need and other questions you may have. Then you find a good seamstress, and of course if you sew yourself then it's all the better. Your custom made garments will be outfits that you can wear many times and can always rely on along with getting the dramatic effect you want. Just look in your closet and see how many garments you have bought on impulse that just sit there not being worn. So please don't worry if you have to spend a little more at times to have your outfits made, they will work for you! And many times they will be cheaper to make! Especially if you take into consideration the time and travel expenses you will save if you go looking for what you want in several fashion stores, which may be endless.

Continue to check with us at: www.namecolorology.com, we are planning on adding the following services for the mass public based on our color philosophy.

Ready to wear mail order catalog • Mail order fabric catalog • Retail fashion stores

We will also be offering an affiliate program on our web site for those who would like to sell our products and services by adding a link from your web site to ours, and receive a percentage of all sales that are generated from your referral.

And for those interested we presently offer a wardrobe and home-decor color/design and consulting service. We also have a fantastic library of glamorous vintage fashion designs from the 20's, 30's, and 40's.

In the future we will be explaining how to use our system to create hundreds of varying image types using your center colors.

We know all of us need new and better ways to give ourselves the edge or advantage to make the difference between success and failure. If you're interested in starting to create a whole new, "make-over", we here at the Name Colorology Group offer several new tools in which to achieve these goals. You can call 1-877-505-9100 or contact us at our web site any time for consultation, for help in this field of expertise.

Chapter 13

PATTERNS AND TEXTURES

Vertical pinstripes will make you look and feel:
Authoritative • Business-like • Decisive • Non deviating • Regal • Taller • Thinner

Flower prints will make you look and feel:
Carefree • Friendlier • Happier • Relaxed • Romantic

Rough thick textures will make you look and feel:
Bolder • Dramatic • Earthier • Masculine • Physical • Warmer • Wider

Smooth thin textures will make you look and feel:
Approachable • Easy going • Suave • Softer • Sophisticated
Feminine • Relaxed • Refined

Light colors will make you look and feel:
Cleaner • Energetic • Friendlier • Happier • Lighter • Wider • Youthful

Medium colors will make you look and feel:
Contemplative • Balanced • Neutral

Dark colors will make you look and feel:
Earthier • Firm • Heavier • Shorter • Opinionated • Serious

Shiny or luster colors and textures will make you look and feel:
Dramatic • Energetic • Glamorous • Sexy

Flat matte colors and textures will make you look and feel:
Conservative • Practical • Relaxed

Chapter 14

JEWELRY AND YOUR CENTER/COLORS

To put it simply, jewelry used with our center/color philosophy is the, "icing on the cake". If you wear your glamorous/sexual center color outfit use glamorous jewelry in that color, if you are using your control/corporate center color outfit use conservative and power jewelry in the same color spectrum for that situation, and so on with the rest of your center/colors. We will be offering a jewelry line that goes along with our system in the future.

Chapter 15

NAME COLOROLOGY PERFUME AND FRAGRANCE PRODUCT LINES

.PERFUME LINE AND FRAGRANCE PRODUCTS

We are also working on a fantastic perfume line along with many fragrance products, soaps, bath salts, candles, incense, soaps, etc.

Chapter 16

OUR COSMETIC LINE

We are presently working on a great cosmetic line that adheres to our color system and will offer a full line of cosmetics. Keep checking with us and we will keep you updated on its progress.

Chapter 17

NUTRITIONAL PRODUCT LINE AND FOOD COLORS

Yes! We also are considering a vitamin and herbal line that will be especially formulated for the seven centers. We also are researching the different color food groups, their beneficial properties, and which foods correlate to the seven centers. Is it a coincidence that there are seven color spectrums, seven energy centers and seven chakra centers?. Do we need the full spectrum of sunlight that contains all the seven colors for optimum well being and a full range of color in our foods? Probably only time and research will tell us. Here is a brief list of some of the different food color groups and some of their benefits. White/flesh color foods: garlic and onions have allyl sulfides that fight cancer. Purple and red/purple foods, such as: raspberries, red wine and other berries that have pholyphenols that fight cancer, red foods such as tomatoes that have lycopene, that have antioxidants and fight cancer. Orange foods such as: carrots and butternut squash that are good for vision and have antioxidants and fight cancer. Yellow and yellow/green foods, such as: mustard greens, kale and collards that can inhibit tumors and help with eyesight. Green foods, such as: brussel sprouts and cabbage that have isothiocyanates, that stimulate enzymes, that round up and eliminate pesticides, toxins and carcinogens, from our bodies, and lastly, blue foods such as, blueberries contain anthocyanins, which are powerful antioxidants.

Chapter 18

Any color combination can work with Gods help, but I have found that certain color combinations work a lot more natural than others, and our color/center traits have a profound effect on how we interact. There are 3 types of chemistry relationships - similarities, opposites, and differentials.

Similar-
Flesh-Flesh
Purple-Purple
Red-Red
Orange-Orange
Yellow-Yellow
Green-Green
Blue-Blue

Opposites-
Purple-Yellow
Red-Green
Orange-Blue
Flesh-Purple
Flesh-Red
Flesh- Orange
Flesh- Yellow
Flesh- Green
Flesh- Blue

Differentials-
Purple-Red
Purple-Orange
Purple-Green
Purple-Flesh
Purple-Blue

Red-Purple
Red-Orange
Red-Yellow
Red-Blue
Red-Flesh

Orange-Purple
Orange-Red
Orange-Yellow
Orange-Green
Orange-Flesh
Flesh-Blue

Yellow- Flesh
Yellow- Red
Yellow- Orange
Yellow- Green
Yellow- Blue

Green-Purple
Green-Orange
Green-Yellow
Green-Flesh
Green- Blue

Blue-Purple
Blue-Red
Blue-Yellow
Blue-Green
Blue-Flesh

Flesh-Purple
Flesh-Red
Flesh-Orange
Flesh-Yellow
Flesh-Green

Here are how the basic color and center types interact. All the color/centers matter but the three I have found to be the most important in helping to create a good relationship, especially a romantic relationship, are spiritual/moral, vocal/harmony, and emotional/romantic.

First, I found spiritual center similar and opposites, to make the most natural and easiest partners, for example: Two orange spiritual people would be the similar type and red and green spiritual people would be opposites.

Second, I found in most cases that differentials have a harder time in their relationships, for example: blue and yellow spiritual people are differential types.

In the case of vocal/harmony center types, I found this center to be very important! I found similar color types in this center to be very harmonious! Why, because they vibrate in the same harmony center color vibration- so simply speaking there will be a natural harmony between them, spirit-body-soul, for example: Da(n)a and Da(n)ny.

Differential and opposites will be less harmonious, especially opposites. I find that opposite vocal/harmony center people have a real hard time being harmonious the majority of the time.

Third I found your emotional/romantic/soul center colors are very important. I found it is usually best to have as many similar emotional center colors so that there is emotional stimulation. For example: two red emotional people.

Another center that can play a major role is the control center, for example: if one person is a red control person and the other a red emotional, then the red control person will have a controlling affect over the red emotional person emotionally. This can have very positive or very negative affects. Have you ever been in a situation in which another person had a very strong controlling affect over you? This situation has to have very careful counseling, guidance, and care.

There are other situations to consider also, for example: one person may be a mental center person operating off their common sense personality and the other person may be an emotional center person operating off of their emotional feelings. Partners that operate off different centers can have many problems. This is another situation that usually needs counseling.
We must also take into consideration if two people have different religions, family backgrounds, astrological differences, ethnic traditions, etc.

You can use your loved one's colors to stimulate them romantically, sexually, or whatever center you want, by wearing their center colors. For example: if your husband's or wife's emotional/romantic center color is a certain red spectrum color wear that color in a soft romantic style and it will have an emotional affect on them. Same with their sexual, etc.

If you are having a lot of disharmony between you and your loved one just try this little bit of advice; start calling each other, "Honey", on a regular bases. This usually has a very helpful affect. By calling each other honey you will be attuning each other to several of your centers, including your harmony center, which I mentioned above. You will also be calling each other by a, "flesh spiritual name", which is the harmony color spectrum, so there should be more harmony in both of your personalities. The well-known fact is that we have associated the name and word of, "honey", to a very positive and sweet image. If calling each other honey does not help matters, or one of you will not agree to call the other honey, there is a another deeper problem occurring from one or more of your seven centers, and these problems need to be brought out in the open and taken care of. For example: maybe one of you has lost a physical attraction to the other or maybe one of you have seen a spiritual moral trait in the other that is a very negative turn-off that is unacceptable and these problems need to be worked on specifically. In many cases we choose partners because we are physically attracted to them or for security reasons, and we don't bother to look at that person's spiritual maturity, later it catches up to us.

To simplify, there are two parts to attraction between people: your physical and your personality. Many times I see two people will have good personality harmony but one or both of them will not be attracted physically, or they like the other persons looks, and can't stand their personality. So what does this tell us? It tells us in order to stand a better chance of being attractive, we must cultivate ourselves spiritually and physically, or better yet, cultivate all your seven centers, and who knows, you may become a 7,8,9 or maybe even a 10 on the attraction scale. You have to work at getting romance just like anything else. To often I see people sitting around watching t.v., or just talking with friends telling them their problems and what they "want". Well, if "you really want it that bad", "you should be willing to work for it". Now remember, I have stated else where in this book that I don't consider myself a charlatan that will tell people anything to make a buck! I try to tell the truth, but sometimes the truth hurts, or some people are not big enough to handle the truth, but it is "truth" that sets you on the path to the right answers and eventually success! So learn how to first face the truth and then do something about it!

Biblical quotes say that we should not choose a mate that is not our equal. So, not only should you cultivate all your seven centers, but you should look for a mate that has also done the same. Often one person is willing to do almost anything to please a mate but the other person is not willing to do hardly anything to help the relationship! What is this telling us? It is telling us that the other person is not interested enough in the person that is willing to do all the work. So, quit trying to force this person to be interested in you and just make yourself the best you can be, that person just may come around and find new interest in you or you can bet some one else will! This is why we should learn to recognize and learn about all the seven centers and what their positive and negative traits are.

I will highly advise again you should have an experienced Name Colorology Group person do an initial reading for relationship name analysis. More times than not I see inexperienced individuals making incorrect readings.

Let me state again anything is possible with God! But why not go with a natural! And make your love relationship much easier!

If you would like a name reading of a love one, potential love one or a example name that would be more harmonious just call us at our toll free number 1-877-505-9100 or contact us at our web site www.namecolorology.com. If you would like counseling on starting a complete "makeover" just give us a call.

Chapter 19

DECORATING YOUR HOME WITH YOUR CENTER/COLORS

How can a person or interior decorator create a relaxed or romantic room environment without knowing the emotional/romantic center colors of the person that will be using that room? Or, how can they create a glamorous sexy environment without knowing a persons glamorous/sexual center colors? We believe, here at the Name Colorology Group, that using the correct colors based on a person's seven centers has a profound affect on those that use this system and individuals and interior decorators should learn our system to create the very best desired room, environment moods. Simply apply your seven center colors to the desired room mood affects that you want to create. Your spiritual colors to stimulate you spiritually and creatively, mental for intellectual stimulation in a study or library, vocal for your harmony, organizing or singing room, physical for a warm, kind, truthful or physical exercising room, control for a formal, power room or business office, emotional for a relaxing, romantic room, and sexual for a glamorous sexy environment. Then determine what period style you like, for example: Antique/Vintage, Art Deco, Art Nouveau, Baroque, Colonial, Country, Creative Art, Egyptian, English, French, Gothic, Greek, Modern, Oriental, Renaissance, Rococo, Romanesque, Romantic, Southwestern, Victorian, etc. Remember to use the type of materials that reflect the mood styles you are creating. How about you parents, would you be interested in what colors relax your kids or stimulate them to study or tap into their creative genius? What about what colors to stimulate your loved one romantically or sexually? We will be producing photographs of individuals in their different center colors in room environments in the future on our website and "our fantastic upcoming magazine" along with other publishing projects: books, calendars, t.v. infomercials, etc. Make sure to get on our mailing list and we will keep you informed on the release of these projects.

Use the home-decor section of the 3-part chart in the back of the book to record your room environment colors; spiritual, mental, vocal, physical, control, emotional and sexual. For consultation you can call us at 1-877-505-9100 or use our web site consulting service at www.name-colorology.com

Chapter 20

MODELS IMAGES IN ADVERTISING

When a company hires a model to represent their product or company image, they almost always pick a model that harmonizes with the message they are sending out. For example: a sexy dress line, they use a sexy model, or what about all the hair product commercials, look at many of the words and messages they send out about their products, clean, sexy, shiny, silky, smooth, soft, wholesome and youthful, and the models they will use will look these parts. Lets get more specific, lets say we have a hair product that makes your hair look soft and romantic, would this company not only want a soft romantic projecting model, and also should she not be wearing her emotional/soft/romantic center color? Yes of course they should if they want to get that "maximum effect".

Chapter 21

TWO GREAT ADVANTAGES OF USING NAME COLOROLGY
IN BUSINESS ADVERTISING

I ask all of you in business how do you expect to get the "maximum effect" out of your advertising if you are using the wrong colors to the images, messages, or words, you are trying to send out to your viewing audience? Imagine a football team using their center in the quarterback position or a baseball team using their power hitter in the 9th spot in the hitting order, or their weakest hitter in the clean up spot! Well, quite simply they're not going to reap the, "maximum benefits", of those players! Now what about the messages and critical points you are trying to send out through brochures, business cards, flyers, logo's, models, packages, signs, or multi-media advertisements, are you using the wrong colors that are not "in tune" with those messages? Ever hear a guitar or piano out of tune? Each color spectrum has a general image it projects. To become more specific, each tint, true hue, and shades of all the spectrums, has it's own character attribute that "it vibrates to" so you can bring the precise words and messages in your ad's to precise harmony with the colors you use! Let me give you a few examples: the word "compassion" vibrates in the rose/pink area, the word "dependable", in the blue spectrum, the word "balance" in the green spectrum and so on. We here at Name Colorology can fine tune all the words and messages you are using in your ad's, to get the "maximum effect" out of the money you are spending on advertising. Getting the right colors to the image message you're wanting to send out, is the first advantage of using our system.

The second great advantage of using Name Colorology is direct mail companies will be able to stimulate each individual in any one of their seven center personality area's. For example: if a company has a creative product, they would want to send out flyers, letters ,etc., to each individual based on that person's spiritual/creative center color and also use certain words based on that person's creative color personality. If a company was selling a emotional/romantic product they would use each individual person's emotional center colors and traits in the mailings and so on with the other center types of products that are geared to them; mental/logical, vocal/harmonious, physical/heart, control/corporate and sexual/survival. The ergonomics of this type of color advertising will be staggering!

"The manufacturer who waits in the woods for the world to beat a path to his door, is a great optimist. But the manufacture who shows his "mouse traps" to the world keeps the smoke coming out of his chimney". - O.B. Winters.

Chapter 22

INCREASING DIRECT CONTACT SALES USING NAME COLOROLOGY

You can increase, and have a much higher success in closing sales, by using Name Colorology just by knowing how to analyze your clients name! How? When you learn the way a person thinks, feels, and what character attributes they consider important, you have a definite advantage! Let me give you a couple examples: Let's say I am an advertising sales person and I am trying to sell a potential client, whose name is William Jones, some advertising space in my magazine. I would definitely be suggesting to this person that he could be creating a good, "image", ad that states how "loyal" and "dedicated" his company is to their customers along with being "honest" and "compassionate"! Why? Because William Jones is a purple and red spiritual person and image, loyalty and dedication are key character traits of purple spiritual people and honesty and compassion are key traits of red spiritual people. This would increase the chance of him to say, "yes I like that kind of thinking", or, "that is a good idea!" I would also make key word trait statements that are in tune with this person's common sense/intellectual, harmony/organizing and control/corporate center color traits. I highly advise that all companies start to pre-analyze all potential clients names before they meet with them so that they better know the ways that person thinks and feels.

"Thank you for the consultation on my interview with the hospital. By using key words, which you gave me, in my interview I received immediate acceptance. Both women were nodding their heads yes to all my answers. The interview went extremely smooth and I left on a very positive note. They did caution me that it might be three weeks before I heard from personnel--but to my surprise, I was called the next week. Knowing what each women was looking for in conversation was extremely effective in guiding the interview to a successful result." Nancy Juliene Frazier

Why not let us here at Name Colorology train your sales people to be able to correctly analyze your clients names for a higher percentage of sales success! 1-877-505-9100 or contact us at www.namecolorology.com

"Business is never so healthy as when, like a chicken, it must do a certain amount of scratching for what it gets". - Henry Ford.

"There are two times in a man's life when he should not speculate: when he can't afford it and when he can". -Samuel Clemens.

Chapter 23

INCREASING WORKER PRODUCTIVITY USING THE NAME COLOROLOGY SYSTEM

Using the Name Colorology system is an excellent way to increase your employees productivity and genius abilities, and at the same time make them more happier and content at their jobs. Do you want to bring out the creative/genius of your workers? Then use their creative, imaginative, spiritual center colors in their workspace and cultivate their spiritual center traits and talents. Do you want them to be more practical and use good common sense? Then their mental center colors will help. Do you want them to project and feel formal and business like? Use their control/corporate center colors. Name Colorology will be used routinely by corporations and governments to gain the upper hand in sales and productivity. Again, the ergonomics of using our system is going to be staggering!

Chapter 24

USING NAME COLOROLOGY TO ACHIEVE FINANCIAL SUCCESS

Anyone can use Name Colorology to achieve financial success! Financial success is not just an ego pleaser: it is a necessity in order to make ends meet nowadays. It means being able to feed and support your family or yourself; so we need to take it serious and make it one of our main priorities. First let me say that I don't consider myself a charlatan or a person that is going to mislead people into believing false statements just to make money off of them. I am not going to make statements such as: if you use our Name Colorology system you will be a millionaire in three or four months! No, I am going to say what I believe is the truth about making money, and I hope and believe most of you will appreciate this honesty. The majority of the time making money involves steady hard work or at least steady work over a period of time, and an, "even better way of looking at it is steady work at what you like doing"! Lets look at what I consider a logical list of how to become financially successful.

1. Working a 9 to 5 job for several years and using simple conservative money management and a savings system, and eventually building a nest egg.

2. Going to college, getting a degree, and being able to command a high salary.

3. Taking a risk by starting your own business, and making financial investments which could fail, or succeed very well, and quite often will take a lot of hard work, time and worry! But as we know, the rewards can be great.

4. Inheriting money or marrying into money, both of which sometimes can be a lot of hard work also.

5. Get lucky by hitting the lotto, etc.

Now looking back again at this list, how can Name Colorology help you to achieve your financial goals? Well, who are we talking about, WE ARE TALKING ABOUT YOU!!! Right! Yes YOU!!!! and who is YOU? REMEMBER THE BIBLICAL QUOTE THAT I MENTIONED IN THE FIRST PART OF THE BOOK --- "KNOW THYSELF" So then is not the first step for you becoming successful at anything just simply, "knowing thyself a little more". So you have started to really know yourself by finding out your character traits and talents from reading the different center/color chapters in this book and determined which centers you have operated and cultivated, along with determining which of the above type you are. Are you the 9 to 5 common-sense/mental center conservative type, or the creative/ spiritual chance taker type? Are you the go to college studious intellectual/mental center type? The corporate/business center type? Are you one of the other center types, vocal, physical, emotional or sexual? Are you an actress, actor, artist, athlete, glamorous sexy model or a singer? No matter which center type you are, you will more than likely have to use and cultivate, to a certain degree, your spiritual/creative, common-sense/mental, vocal/organizing and control/business centers. Another part of succeeding is to determine if you are selling a service, a product, or both. I know it sounds rather simple, but simple formula's work quite well. Name Colorology has quite a lot of knowledge of who you are! I usually advise that a person go with a career that is attuned to their spiritual/creative/genius center, but not always. I also take into consideration the persons whole name, background, experience and what center they operate off most or if they are a double center color person and other personality influencing factors and environmental factors etc. Remember we are talking about you! You are an individual, a one of a kind, so I believe each person needs to be individually analyzed. Remember you have been called your name thousands of times which has had a major affect on your personality and talents. Let me say, in all honesty, if someone were to ask me, "If I, just read your book, will I know for sure what my career choices should be?" I would say, "Possibly!" But I would strongly advise you getting that initial reading by calling the Name Colorology Group for several reasons. Ok, so some of you are saying "sure so you can get more money out of me!" I truly believe, that most, need the additional help and besides, we are very reasonable in our fee's along with being very good at what we do. We will give at least three excellent career choices and we can give you more but we really like to focus on no more than three. How much is your career worth to you? Quite a bit isn't it! Your career and the money you make from it determines much of the rest of how your life will be! Whether you can buy the house you want, the car you want the vacations you want, the way you want to be able to support your children and if you can send them to college!! SO GET SERIOUS AND GET FOCUSED ABOUT YOUR CAREER AND MONEY-MAKING ABILITIES!

 I also highly advise you to get in touch with your control/corporate and harmony/organizational center colors and traits for good business and organizing skills along with projecting these traits to others.

How many times have we seen or heard famous successful people being interviewed and asked to give the listeners their one bit of best key advice to succeeding, and what do they almost always say, "KEEP TRYING!" In chapter 28 of this book I explain my systems to cultivating your centers and my key advice is "repetitive-ness" which in other words is "keep trying"--DON'T FORGET TO READ THIS CHAPTER!

Succeeding is like breaking down a huge boulder with a sledgehammer and chisel. Your not going break it down with one hit or two or three, your going to chip it down bit by bit, day by day, a little at a time, and it is the "repetitive-ness" that will make you succeed!

Ok, now let's say you have determined what career is your best choice and you have cultivated or developed your service or product that you want to sell to others. The last three steps to succeeding financially are, learning to "sell", "market" and maintain your service or product! These are very important. There are a lot of talented people out there that have good idea's, products or services yet they lack the sales, marketing and organizing skills. If you lack these skills the logical way to acquire them is simple, learn how to do these your self or have others do them for you! If you decide to cultivate them yourself, especially if you can't afford to hire others, (If you have to seek financial backing you will still need to learn how to sell and market yourself to those that will fund your project). There are many books and services that explain the in's and out's of "how to." So which one's do you buy or use? Let me say the best way is to shop around and compare-believe me, don't jump onboard with the first one you come into contact with. You can go on the internet and type in what you're looking to do with the different search engines and you will get a very good variety, for example let"s say your a artist trying to market your work . You can start by typing in "marketing art" or "how to market a artist" into a search engine and you will probably get quite a few sites that specalize in that field. You will be surprised also at how many books are available on marketing and selling just about any thing out there. You can also call our toll free 1-877-505-9100 number or use our email service at www.namecolorology.com and we can help you at our very reasonable rates. We have a lot of excellent resources, tips, and experience in these fields. We also have an excellent affiliate program if you would like to make money referring customers from your web site to our site by adding a "click on" link on your web page. We pay an excellent percentage rate of all sales made by customers that were referred from your site.

The musician, the painter, and the poet, are in a larger sense, no greater artists than the man of commerce. - W. S. Maverick

Success or failure in business is caused more by the mental attitude than by mental capacities. - Walter Dill Scott.

Chapter 25

NAME COLOROLOGY AND THE ENTERTAINMENT INDUSTRY

I ask how can an actress or actor playing an emotional/romantic part, project that image not wearing their emotional center color, or a youthful, wholesome, cheerful part wearing their control or sexual center colors? It definitely takes away from the image they are trying to convey! Look at our models in this book, do they not, "look the image," we are claiming? I have seen many times when individuals are trying to project an image with the wrong colors and it is a shame to see it weakened so much by this mistake. The entertainment industry is an excellent field in which to use the Name Colorology system! **We presently offer an exclusive evening gown design service for gala events and will be opening a exclusive wardrobe/home-decor store and beauty salon in the Los Angeles area**. We also have plans to open other boutiques in many major cities in the U.S. and around the world.

Chapter 26

ARTISTS - YOUR COLORS AND THE COLORS FOR YOUR CLIENTS

Name Colorology is a great "tool" for artists who want to create pieces of art for themselves and for their clients. If you want to create art that is in tune with your own personality, use your center colors to create the mood art you want.

Here is a basic list of how you can use colors for your self:

Your spiritual center colors can be used to create very spiritual, moral, creative, imaginative, happy, clean, cheerful, and fun pieces of art that will stimulate you in these ways. As for your clients, you have to take into consideration their spiritual center colors or the colors that pertain to the message of their business images and messages.

Your mental center colors can be used to create intellectual pieces of art for yourself and your clients for personal or business uses.

Your vocal center colors can be used to create very harmonious works of art or a message of unity or organization, and depending on the uses of your clients personal or business related.

Your physical center colors can be used to create very warm, kind, giving, truthful messages and moods. Again when it comes to your clients you have to consider their physical center colors for personal or business products they are advertising. You can also create very dramatic pieces of art using your heart center colors.

Your control center colors can be used to stimulate you to create all the traits attuned to the control center: formal, in-control, empowerment, regality, dignity, and corporate. By learning the Name Colorology system you can create these images for your clients for personal or business uses.

Your emotional center colors can help stimulate you to create soulful, romantic, relaxed, or contented art for yourself or others.

Your sexual center colors can help you to create glamorous, sexy or earthy works of art for you and others.

For consultation for artists, graphic artists, potters or any other artistic professionals call our toll free number 1-877-505-9100 or contact our web site www.namecolorology.com

Chapter 27

CHANGING YOUR NAME TO ACQUIRE NEW CHARACTER TRAITS, TALENTS, CAREERS, RELATIONSHIPS OR OTHER USES

Would you like to become a writer, or increase your abilities if you already are one? Would you like to become an artist, architect, designer, doctor, lawyer, singer or any other career field you are interested in? You can greatly improve your chances of doing so by choosing the right name that supports any career you would like to excel in. Would you like a better relationship with someone in your life, love one, relative, co-worker or friend? Make sure, for career choice names, to read the center color chapter that pertains to the career of interest and for relationships make sure to read the chapter before this one. For a custom designed name for any career or relationship just call us or contact our web site.

Chapter 28

CULTIVATING YOUR SEVEN CENTERS

Here are some simple and practical steps to cultivating your seven centers, and remember, repeat these daily because it is this repeating action that will play a major part in making these positive traits to become a regular part of your personality. We have all heard the expression, " practice makes perfect," and do not take this saying lightly, it really works!

"Great things are done by a series of small things brought together."-Vincent Van Gogh

SPIRITUAL CENTER

Your spiritual center, as stated earlier, is where your moral conscience originates. So, if you are lacking good morals then you need to cultivate this center. The best way to start to cultivate this center is check your conscience and ask yourself if you are hurting other people by your actions. Are other people regularly telling you that you lack morals? Are you going against societies laws of morality, are you mean spirited, cruel, dishonest, selfish or constantly trying to force your will on others? If you're being immoral, than the best way to start to correct this problem is: the very next time you are confronted with a moral decision of right and wrong make the right decision, remember this first time is the start to conditioning yourself to creating a new habit! Creating a new good habit that will replace the old bad one with a new better addiction! Break that ice the first time! Then continue the "One time at a time one day at a time" system of doing this, before you know it you will have a week , a month, a year, of good habit and you will be on your way to creating a new better person! Remember it is the repetition as much as anything that will be the key to your success! Learn also to laugh at things in life instead of taking everything too seriously. That also takes the ability to have faith in God and if you follow his teachings, things will work out and free you from worry, guilt, stress, unhappiness and a downgraded spirit! Then you will have a clean, guilt free, wholesome, and youthful appearance and personality. Your spiritual center will be energized and ready to have more fun and happiness in your life. Your spiritual center will also be clean and open to become more imaginative and creative. God wants us to be creative and productive. He has given all of us the ability of creative genius; he wants us to be like him! God gave us our spiritual center for these reasons. God gave each and every one of us our own moral temple when he gave us our spiritual center. He also gave us all free will to make our own moral decisions of right and wrong, so when you take it upon yourself to cultivate your spiritual center, you will be able to choose the right spiritual path for yourself. Remember the simple but very true sayings, "let your conscience be your guide", "do on to others as you would have others do on to you", and "whoever has not sinned cast the first stone". Also, always remember, Jesus died for our sins so we could have a new, eternal, clean, wholesome, creative, loving, life with God and our fellow brothers, sisters and creatures of heaven and earth. If you still have unanswered questions on cultivating your spiritual center nature, ask your pastor, priest, read the bible, or ask those you consider to be of a good moral nature their opinion. Just be careful not to let anyone force their spiritual will on you, in which you do not feel completely comfortable or feel a clear conscience! Remember to read and cultivate your spiritual center color traits and talents that God gave you through your name! "Know thyself." Who are you? A lot of who you are, is in your name!

SAYINGS THAT STIMULATE OUR SPIRITUAL CENTER:

Man's conscience is the oracle of God. - Byron

A good conscience is the palace of Christ: the temple of the Holy Ghost: the paradise of delight: the standing Sabbath of the saints. - Augustine

He hath a poor spirit who is not planted above petty wrongs. - Feltham.

A man of right spirit is not a man of narrow and private views, but is greatly interested and concerned for the community to which he belongs, and particularly of the city or village in which he resides, and for the true welfare of the society of which he is a member. - Jonathan Edwards.

He that loseth wealth, loseth much: he that loseth friends, loseth more: but he that loseth his spirit, loseth all. - Spanish Maxim

Conscience is merely our own Judgment of the right or wrong of our actions, and so can never be a safe guide unless enlightened by the word of God. - Tryon Edwards

A good conscience is the palace of Christ: the temple of the Holy Ghost: the paradise of delight: the standing Sabbath of the saints. - Augustine

It is far more important to me to preserve an unblemished conscience than to compass any object however great. - Channing

Genius may be described as the spirit of discovery. - It is the eye of intellect, and the wing of thought, - It is always in advance of its time the pioneer for the generation which it precedes. - Simms

When a true genius appears in the world, you may know him by this sign that the dunces are all in confederacy against him. - Swift

The first and last thing required of genius is the love of truth. - Goethe

Genius fins its own road, and carries its own lamp. - Willmott

Talent, lying in the understanding, is often inherited; genius, being the action of reason and imagination, rarely or never. -annonymous

MENTAL CENTER

The first step in cultivating your intellectual/mental center is FIRST, cultivate your spiritual center so you can make good moral intellectual decisions! Your mental center is your analytical logical center for making logical correct decisions in simple and complex situations. The next time you have a simple or non emergency problem, question or task you do not know the answer to, sit down and say to yourself, "what is the logical way to try to figure this out?" Clear your mind and start to analyze it slowly one step at a time and tell yourself, "I can figure this out if I take my time and use logic!" The more that you try to use your logical mind the more it will eventually respond. We have all heard the expression that, "the mind is the biggest muscle of your body and the more you exercise it, the bigger it will get"! This saying is very true! Don't be mentally lazy every time you run into something you do not know the answer to! Try to figure it out! Use that logical center that God gave you!!! Cultivate it! Start working that muscle. Before you know it you will start to gain more confidence in being able to figure out how to solve simple and eventually more complex problems. How do you think those brainy professors and scientists got so smart; they read and analyzed over and over again, they worked their brain muscle just as a weight lifter works his body muscles! They cultivated their mental center that God gave them! Remember, start with small non critical situations. If you do not have the time or it is an important critical problem, what is the most logical answer to the problem? Yes, seek an experts advice! The other function of the mental center is using good common sense, for example: if you have a friend that is always getting into trouble, should you be hanging around them? No! Why, because their bad habits could get you into trouble even if you are not the one causing trouble. Use good common sense and get away from that person! Are you making your decisions emotionally versus using common sense? Stop using your emotional center when you should use your mental center! If you're just coming down with a cold or flu should you go out with a friend that wants to have a good time? No! You will just compound that illness and make the recovery time longer and miss a greater time at work and lose a lot of wages! Should you become intimate with someone you just met? No! Get to know that person, like they say, it takes time to really know a person! Just good old common sense knowledge; learn to use it!

SAYINGS THAT STIMULATE OUR MENTAL CENTER:

If common sense has not the brilliancy of the sun, it has the fixity of the stars. - Caballero

The crown of all faculties is common sense. It is not enough to do the right thing; it must be done at the right time and place. Talent knows what to do; tact knows when and how to do it. - W. Matthews

Common sense is, of all kinds, the most uncommon. It implies good judgment, sound discretion, and true and practical wisdom applied to common life. - Tryon Edwards

To act with common sense according to the moment, is the best wisdom I know. The best philosophy is to do one's duties, take the world as it comes, submit respectfully to one's lot, bless the goodness that has given us so much happiness with it, whatever it is, and despise affectation. - Walpole

If a man can have only one kind of sense let him have common sense. If he has that and uncommon sense too, he is not far from genius. - H.G. Beecher

One pound of learning requires ten pounds of common sense to apply it. - Persian Proverb

Common sense is the knack of seeing things as they are, and doing things as they ought to be done. - C.E. Stowe

The intellect of the wise is like glass, it admits the light of heaven and reflects it. - Hare

If we would guide by the light of reason, we must let our minds be bold. - Justice Brandeis

The mind grows narrow in proportion as the soul grows corrupt. - Rousseau

Never reason from what you do not know. If you do, you will soon believe what is utterly against reason. - Ramsay

If a man's eye is on the eternal, his intellect will grow. - Emerson

As the soil, however rich it may be, cannot be productive without culture, so the mind without cultivation can never produce good fruit. - Seneca

What stubbing, plowing, digging, and harrowing is to land, that thinking, reflecting, examining is to the mind. Each has its proper culture; as the land that is suffered to lie waste and wild for a long time will be overspread with brushwood, brambles, and thorns, which have neither use nor beauty, so there will not fail to sprout up in a neglected, uncultivated mind. A great number of prejudices and absurd opinions, which owe their origin partly to the soil itself, the passions, and imperfections of the mind of man, and partly to those seeds which chance to be scattered in it by every wind of doctrine which the cunning of statesmen, the singularity of pedants, and superstition of fools shall rise. - Berkeley

True wisdom is to know what is best worth knowing, and to do what is best worth doing.
- Humphrey

VOCAL/HARMONY CENTER

Cultivating your vocal/harmony center is very important in all aspects of your life primarily in singing, getting along with others in a pleasant harmonious manner and getting your life organized in all areas. Again whatever application of this center you want to cultivate singing, harmony or organization the same rule applies Repetition! One time at a time one day at a time! The very next time you are faced with a argument with another person stop yourself (you will also need to cultivate your control center to apply this trait) and say I am going to be pleasant and not argue with this person! I am going to be harmonious! prepare your self when you are going to be around someone you know is not harmonious, do this repeatedly. Soon you will start to see that you can become more pleasant and harmonious on a regular basis. Remember you must do this repeatedly for it to become a natural habit of your personality! To cultivate organization and unity in your life you need to learn the functions of all the seven centers and bring them all into balance and harmony, (look at our general signs of excessive use of centers and general signs of lack of use of centers sections in the following sections of this chapter) On a daily basis upon the end of the day ask your self what center do I need to work on tomorrow and what do I need to do most tomorrow to bring harmony into my life and make it a priority and do it! eventually following the "one time at a time one day at a time" system you will create a more organized and harmonious person of your self! The vocal center is also a reflection of the rest of our centers, for instance: if we are in a very emotional mood our voice will sound very emotional. If we are in a very cheerful spiritual mood our voice will vibrate to a cheerful sound and as we all know, certain ethnic people are conditioned to talk in certain ethnic styles which are sometimes very nasal or very guttural that effect their vocal center. Breathing also effects our vocal sounds.

If you want to sound intellectual and practical align your mental center with your vocal center by concentrating on deriving your thoughts and sounds from these two centers. A person who talks with a lot of physical gestures is aligning one's physical center with one's vocal center. A person who talks in a very spirited manner is aligning one's spiritual and vocal centers. Decide on how you wish to sound or project, and concentrate on that center while speaking.

SAYINGS THAT STIMULATE OUR VOCAL CENTER:

There is no index of character so sure as the voice. - Tancred

How sweetly sounds the voice of a good woman! When it speaks it ravishes all senses. - Massinger

Never is the deep, strong voice of man, or the low, sweet voice of woman, finer than in the earnest but mellow tones of familiar speech, richer, than the richest music, which are a delight while they are heard, which linger still upon the ear in softened echoes, and which when they have ceased, come, long after, back to memory, like the murmurs of a distant hymn.
- Henry Giles

The sound must seem an echo to the sense. - Pope

To a nice ear the quality of a voice is singularly affecting. Its depth seems to be allied to feeling: at least the contralto notes alone give an adequate sense of pathos. They are born near the heart. - Tuckerman

How deep is the magic of sound may be learned by breaking some sweet verses into prose. The operation has been compared to gathering dewdrops, which shine like jewels upon the flower, but run into water in the hand. The elements remain, but the sparkle is gone. - Willmott

There is in souls a sympathy with sounds, and as the wind is pitched the ear is pleased with melting airs or martial, brisk or grave: Some chord in unison with what we hear is touched within us, and the heart replies.- Cowper

PHYSICAL /HEART CENTER

Cultivating the different functions of your physical/heart center again is based on repetition and being a good moral person! This center has two basic functions staying in good physical condition and the ability to have a good, honest, warm, kind, giving heart! Lets start with the kind heart. As I stated with the other previous centers, the next time you're confronted with a decision to be honest, kind, warm, compassionate or giving, versus being dishonest, cruel, cold, uncompassionate or stingy, make the right decision and have a good kind heart! Then the time after that do it again! Remember: one time at a time, one day at a time! The more you do it, the more it will become a natural part of your personality. I know this seems very simple but there is so much knowledge in simplicity, and simple techniques work so well if you follow them, so please do not disregard the effectiveness of simple formulas. People look for that so often heard quote "the quick fix" or the "magical solution" to occur, well I have seen more and better results happen to people who are willing to have patience and use good simple practical systems. Now how do we cultivate our physical bodies? Well, we have all heard many times good nutritious eating habits and exercise on a regular basis. I can think of no better example of my one time at a time, one day at a time system, than now! Just look at body builders who lift weights 3 to 4 times a week, what happens to their muscles? They get bigger and they get stronger! They become more toned and in shape! So goes it with all our seven centers; the more we exercise them the stronger they get! If you go to a gym one day, do not think you will come out looking like Mr. or Ms. America, you won't! Yet it will be a start, and if you follow a 3 to 4 day a week one day at a time routine at home or in a gym you will surely start to see a much better toned and shaped body! It is fairly well proven that exercise leads to a healthier heart and stronger immune system! I have found that you do not have to exercise in any extreme manner, just keep it moderate! Again, check with your doctor before doing any physical exercises. The second part of cultivating a good healthy body is what you eat. I personally use a vegetarian diet (with enough b12 vitamin), with lots of good organic vegetables, fruits, moderate grains and protein with added vitamins and minerals. I also use what I call a "body set point" system that works very well. I have studied nutrition, herbs and vitamins for many years and will be coming out with a physical exercise and nutrition book hopefully in the near future that will also include nutrition for the seven centers and my system on losing and keeping weight off. Continue to check my web site, namecolorology.com for any new products or services. Again, before changing any of your eating habits check with your doctor!

SAYINGS THAT STIMULATE OUR PHYSICAL/HEART CENTER:

Be noble-minded! Our own heart and not other men's opinions of us, forms our true honor.
- Schiller

The wise, for cure, on exercise depend. Better to hunt in fields for health unbought than fee the doctor for a nauseous draught. - Dryden.

Health is the vital principle of bliss; and exercise, of health. - Thomson

The only way for a rich man to be healthy is by exercise and abstinence, to live as if he was poor; which are esteemed the worst parts of poverty. - Sir W. Temple

Inactivity, supine-ness, and effeminacy have ruined more constitutions than were ever destroyed by excessive labors. Moderate exercise and toil, so far from prejudicing, strengthen and consolidate the body. - Richard Rush

CONTROL CENTER

Cultivating your control center is one of the most important parts of succeeding in any endeavor in your life. I call this center many names such as, the control, corporate, empowerment, regal, dignity, business, formal, fight or flight, and anti-addiction center. I also refer to it as the "boss" center and if you have problems controlling any bad habits, you need to make it the boss center in your personality! What are two words we hear when a person is talking about their or another person's addiction or bad habit? The word "control" such as "I can't seem to control it", or, "he or she can't seem to control them self", "I can't seem to control my drinking or my drug habit or my temper," or whatever negative addiction a person has! The word "change" such as "I need to change my habit," or, "That person needs to make some changes in their life" The words "control" and "change", seem to be there! Those are the "key" words to overcoming these bad addictions! Simply stated, a bad addiction needs to be "controlled" and "changed" to a new good addiction and what better center could a person use to do this than their "control center". Let it take control of your centers till you learn! Let it become the, "dominate center in your personality"! God gave you a control center for a purpose so why not use it when needed? The very next time you are faced with a situation when you need to control a bad habit let your, power control center say, "No, I am the boss this time and I am not going to give in". Let it be dominate over all the other centers that are saying, "but I want to do this", whether it is your emotional or sexual or any other center trying to make the decision don't let them let your control center be the one to make the decision, let it be boss for a day! That is when you will start to cultivate your control center! Your center of being dignified and able to say to yourself and others I controlled myself and then your self-esteem will start to grow! Remember the, "one time at a time one day at a time" system! The more you do this the stronger your control center will become! Your control center is also your civil and culture center so when you start to cultivate it use these words to yourself such as, "I am going to be more civil, cultured and dignified", and they will help you to tune into this center! To cultivate the business/career function of this center I will use a very old, but what may be the best saying of them all when it comes to business, " BUSINESS BEFORE PLEASURE"! So in other words, "if you are putting emotional feelings and other pleasures ahead of taking care of business, you need to switch the centers you operate off of!" START CULTIVATING THAT CONTROL BUSINESS CENTER!

SAYINGS THAT STIMULATE OUR CONTROL CENTER:

Who to himself is law, no law doth need.- Chapman

No conflict is so severe as his who labors to subdue himself.- Thomas A. Kempis

It is the man who is cool and collected, who is master of his countenance, his voice, his actions, his gestures, of every part, who can work upon others at his pleasure. - Diderot

No man is free who cannot command himself. - Pythagoras

Self-respect, - that cornerstone of all virtue. - Sir John Herscal

To business that we love, we rise betimes, and go to it with delight. - Shakespeare.

The art of winning in business is in working hard- not taking it too seriously. - Elbert Hubbard.

EMOTIONAL CENTER

Cultivating your emotional/romantic center is also a matter of controlling it! Why, because emotional feelings are very powerful! They can overcome us very easily if we don't learn to control them, at the same time we have to learn when to release them! It is said by some that "love is the most powerful force in the universe" and we all want love! It can make an angry person peaceful, a discontented person content, and a sad person happy. It can make all the difference in the world! Women know this more than anyone! Most young people are controlled by their emotions and have to go through that painful period of controlling them as they age, or we can use the word mellowing or maturing our emotions. To cultivate your emotional center you have to learn who and what is worth getting emotional over or who really likes us emotionally and who does not. A person also has to learn how to communicate their emotions and feelings in a personal mature way, and how to be a little more personal in the way they communicate their feelings. It takes being able to expose a little bit of your romantic soul, or feelings because your emotional center is your "soul" center and your soul is where you get your feelings from! God has told us our soul and our spirit, are everlasting. God gave us our soul to be able to "feel". Could you imagine not having any feelings? If we did not have any feelings we might as well be a cold slab of steel! How incredibly boring life would be! God gave us our spirit to have faith that we will be loved and we will feel love as never before when we reach heaven, and he has told us we can feel and give love here on earth! I may not be able to explain in the best of words about the soul and love, but God knows what he was doing when he gave us our souls, and whatever God does he has a very important and beautiful plan for us! A plan that includes wonderful feelings of love, contentment and joy! So the next time you are faced with showing some kind personal emotional feelings to a loved one, friend, animal or advocate, do so! Show them you recognize and are doing what God wanted you to do to be able to love! Remember, "Jesus said if you do but one thing on this earth let it be to love one another"!

Again, as stated in the other centers, "one time at a time one day at a time", keep doing it and you will become a more soulful loving person and it will make you more loveable and others will be more loveable to you. Remember, there is the right time and place for everything. Do not try to force your love on someone that does not have as strong feelings towards you, let them love who they want. God gave us all free will, and if you are trying to force your will on someone else you are interfering with that God given gift of free will!

150

Our emotional center is what I also call the, relax /contentment center because when a person is able to find or give love they become contented and relaxed. Have you ever heard the expression, "I don't care what happens," "I'm in Love"? Try laying down on a bed when you don't feel contented or loved and breath very slowly to your abdomen were your emotion center is located, and say to yourself I can give love and I am loved! God loves me and he will make sure that I am loved if I give love, and have faith in his love too, and at this very moment I am contented and overwhelmed with love, and whenever love comes my way I will except it and let it fill my soul with absolute joy and contentment! Another good exercise to make your emotional center feel at ease is to practice breaking into a good soulful belly laugh! Do you remember how good those make you feel?

SAYINGS THAT STIMULATE OUR EMOTIONAL CENTER:

It is a beautiful necessity of our nature to love something.- Jerrold.

The greatest pleasure of life is love.- Sir W. Temple.

There comes a time when the souls of human beings. Women more even than men, begin to faint for the atmosphere of the affections they are made to breathe. - O. W. Holmes.

The heart of him who truly loves God is a paradise on earth; he has God in himself,
for God is love.- Lamennais.

Resign every forbidden joy; restrain every wish that is not referred to God's will; banish all eager desires, all anxiety; desire only the will of God; seek him alone and supremely, and you
will find peace. - Fenelon

If you are but content you have enough to live upon with comfort.- Plautus

The taste for emotion may become a dangerous taste; we should be very cautious how we attempt to squeeze out of human life more ecstasy and paroxysm that it can well afford.
- Sydney Smith

A contented mind is the greatest blessing a man can enjoy in this world; and if, in the present life, his happiness arises from the subduing of his desires, it will arise in the next from the gratification of them. - Addison

Alternate rest and labor long endure. - Ovid

Emotion, whether of ridicule, anger, or sorrow, whether raised at a puppet show, a funeral, or a battle, is your grandest of levelers. The man who would be always superior should be
always apathetic. - Bulwer

Submission is the only reasoning between a creature and its maker and contentment in his will is the best remedy we can apply to misfortunes. - Sir W. Temple
Emotion turning back on itself, and not leading on to thought or action, is the element of madness.- J. Sterling

151

It is right to be contented with what we have, never with what we are.- MacKintosh

There are pauses amidst study, and even pauses of seeming idleness, in which a process goes on which may be likened to the digestion of food. In those seasons of repose, the powers are gathering their strength for new efforts; as land which lies fallow recovers itself for tillage. - J.W. Alexander

By starving emotions we become humorless, rigid and stereotyped; by repressing them we become literal, reformatory and holier-than-thou; encouraged, the perfume life; discouraged, they poison it.
- Dr. Joseph Collins

I never complained of my condition but once, said an old man "when my feet were bare, and I had no money to buy shoes; but I met a man without feet, and became contented". - annonymous

All work and no rest takes the spring and bound out of the most vigorous life. -Time spent in judicious resting is not time wasted, but time gained. - M.B. Grier

All loving emotions, like plants, shoot up most rapidly in the tempestuous atmosphere of life. - Richter

The contented man is never poor; the discontented never rich. He who is not contented with what he has, would not be contented with what he would like to have. - annonymous

Ride your emotions as the shallow rides the waves; don't get upset among them. There are people who enjoy getting swamped emotionally just as incredibly, there are people who enjoy getting drunk. - Mary Austin

Contentment is natural wealth, luxury is artificial poverty. - Socrates

Rest is not quitting the busy career; rest is the fitting of self to its sphere. - J. Dwight

SEXUAL CENTER

The first step in cultivating your sexual center is to get in touch with the area of your body where your sexual center is located, and start to study the functions of this center. The best way to get in touch with your sexual center is to plant your feet and start to do a little hip swaying exercise from side to side. If we stop to study famous, glamorous, sexy people they always seem to have that sexy, suave, smooth hip swagger in their walk and movements. You will also notice they usually slow their speech down and draw out their words in a patient, sexy, suave manner. They also have an earthy confidence that is seductive in nature, a kind of, "well this is who I am and I am worthy of attention," at the same time not giving or trying to prove themselves very hard, and creating that air of mystery and confidence in what they can do.

Our sexual center is also our survival center and grounding center. Those that are usually the sexy type are survivors and no how to ground themselves and say, "ok, here I am and this is what I have to do to survive theses hard times". These are the types you can't usually, "pull the wool over their eyes", as the saying goes, or "your not going to fool me" type!

Our sexual center is also our reproductive center. It has been proven that when a person of the opposite sex views a potential mate they tend to pick those that are in very good shape, or successful financially. This sends out a message that they would be able to create good healthy children along with being able to take care of them. So what have we stated so far? Suave, smooth, slow, seductive, mysterious, confident, healthy, grounded, and an air that they can take care of themselves in tough times.

Now, getting back to the exercise of swaying your hips side to side in a suave, slow, fluid, seductive manner, and why not turn the lights down low and put on a little quite sexy music. Now you're getting the idea! As you continue to do this start to move your neck in a slow circular motion, get your body in a fluid mode and you can even start to make soft low slow sexy little sounds, don't you dare laugh! This is working, is it not? Are you not feeling a whole lot sexier? Now say to yourself, "the next time I go out anywhere, I am going to walk and talk slower, in a patient, fluid, suave, sexier, seductive and confident manner!" Remember, you do not have to do this in a extreme manner, just enough to get the message out that you're a little steamy, mildly steamy. Pull them in, don't push them away! Again, I will say, "practice", repeat this exercise, the more you do it the more you will learn the right degree and ingredients to make yourself a slightly smooth, creamy, seductive mouth watering piece of cake! Remember, it is the repetition of actions that make us become whatever we repeat. So, if you want to be sexy, repeat these exercises one time at a time one day at a time!

SEXUAL SAYINGS:

The principal reason for sex deification is loss of belief of God. Once men lose God, they lose the purpose of life; and when the purpose of living is forgotten, the universe becomes meaningless. Man then tries to forget his emptiness in the intensity of a momentary experience.
- Fulton J. Sheen

Sex is as much psychological as physical. Certainly love is much more than physical sex appeal. - Harold H. Titus

Sex has become one of the most discussed subjects of modern time. The Victorians pretended it did not exist; the moderns pretend that nothing else exists. - Fulton J. Sheen

Chapter 29

GENERAL SIGNS OF EXCESSIVE USE OF CENTERS

Spiritual- Spiritually open to too many philosophies, spreading oneself to thin with too many creative ideas, being gullible and trying to be too friendly with everyone.

Mental- Mental confusion, scattered minded, overly analytical, mental exhaustion.

Vocal- Hoarse or lost voice from yelling. Trying to organize to extreme or unrealistic detail.

Physical- Prone to physical injuries, broken bones, sprained ankles and injuries in general, too aggressive and dramatic.

Control- Too snobbish, power hungry, petty criticisms and controlling.

Emotional- Emotional breakdown, excessive crying, upset stomach, overly emotional, falling in love to easily or quickly and not being able to relax or be contented.

Sexual- Sexual perversions, sexual malfunctions, diseases.

Chapter 30

GENERAL SIGNS OF TOO LITTLE USE OF CENTERS

Spiritual- No spiritual beliefs, narrow mindedness, lack of spirit, feeling old, unimaginative, violent philosophies and lacking moral conscience.

Mental- Dumbfounded, scattered, inability to be logical, analytical or practical.

Vocal- Not being able to feel or be harmonious, lacking the ability to express oneself verbally and lacking organization skills.

Physical- Out of shape, poor muscle tone, inability to be truthful, forgiving or compassionate.

Control- Lack of control, impulsive buying, eating or other impulsive habits, excessive alcohol or drug habits, lack of power, and dignity (self-respect).

Emotional- Too impersonal, inability to communicate emotionally, lacking romantic feelings.

Sexual- Sexual frigidity, lack of sexual interest and sexual dysfunction's, not being grounded enough to meet life's challenges.

Chapter 31

THE INCREDIBLE ENDOCRINE GLANDS THEORY

During my research and studies of the 7 energy centers I discovered that these centers, (Spiritual, Mental, Vocal, Physical, Control, Emotional and Sexual), were located in the same general areas of the 7 chakra centers, (Crown, Brow, Throat, Heart, Solar Plexus, Navel and Root). This was described by eastern philosophies and a little later noticed they were also located in the same areas of our 7 major endocrine glands. The more I studied these 7 energy centers I became increasingly aware that people seemed to operate off of, and cultivate some of the centers more than others. Then it made me think if a person is in the habit of operating off of a particular center would it not be possible for them to be releasing hormones from the endocrine gland located in that center area? Then I thought, well we've always been told that repetition creates habit and habit creates addiction. So, if we are possibly releasing hormones from an endocrine gland that is in the area of the center we are operating off of, then would we not become hormonally addicted to that particular endocrine gland secretions? For example, if a person has operated off of their control center most of the time, would it not be possible that that person is routinely releasing and becoming addicted to their adrenal gland hormones? Or a person operating off of their mental/analytical center becoming addicted to their pituitary endocrine gland hormones? Then I thought this could also be the reason why we find it so hard to change our habits. For example, take a person that operates off of their emotional center most of the time in making most of their decisions. They realize later, saying to themselves, or by others, "should have used more common sense", or, "you should use your mind versus your emotions in certain situations", or even, "should learn how to control yourself". In other words you should get in the habit of operating and cultivating your mental and control centers. Well, almost all of us have habits we truly realize and want to change and try to change but seem to fall back to our old habits, true? I suspect that the reason why it is so hard to change our habits is because we may be hormonally addicted to our own hormones depending on which centers we repeatedly operate off of.

Again I will say, this is only a theory which needs to be proved or disproved and you should check with a qualified physician before using any new formulas, etc.

I also believe we can become addicted to certain character attributes, for example: being uncompassionate versus compassionate, undependable versus dependable or arrogant versus modest. Now how do we change any negative habits or cultivate and operate off a different center?

Chapter 32

CHANGING OUR HABITS AND CENTERS

I have a very simple 3-part formula for changing negative habits, addictions etc.

1. Awareness and Admitting- Awareness and admitting to your negative habits is the first step, if you are not aware or in denial this will be the first road block to changing your habits so become aware and quit denying that you need to change!

2. Learning the functions and jobs of your 7 centers and which ones you need to cultivate more and which ones you need to change. For example, if you are being immoral and lack a good moral conscience than you need to start to operate and cultivate your moral/spiritual center more. If you lack control over negative addictions (smoking, drugs, alcohol, impulsive, shopping, etc.) or make most of your decisions emotionally versus good common sense, then you need to start to cultivate your control and mental centers. Remember: we almost always hear others or say to ourselves, "I want to change or quit but I just can't seem to control it." God gave us these centers for a reason so we need to show God that we appreciate them and cultivate them all.

Spiritual Center ---For getting in touch with our God given moral conscience, making the right moral decisions, having faith in God and becoming more creative in solving our problems along with uplifting our spirits.

Mental Center ---For using our intellect, analytical skills and good common sense.

Vocal/Harmonious Center---For communicating, organizing and bringing our centers into a mind-body-soul harmonious unity for becoming a more pleasant, harmonious person towards ourselves and others.

Physical/Heart Center--- For being honest, compassionate, forgiving, and for staying in good physical shape.

Control/Business Center--- For controlling our actions, having dignity, will power, and taking care of business and our responsibilities.

Emotional/Romantic Center--- For having the ability to have feelings for others and realizing others have feelings too, along with being able to love and to learn to be a contented relaxed human being.

Sexual/Grounding/Survival Center--- For reproducing and co-creating as God told us to do along with grounding ourselves and learning how to survive our present situations.

3. One day at a time, repetition, and patience- Realize that repetition is the main ingredient to creating habit, either good or bad. If you have been in the repetitious habit of operating off of a negative habit, or off of a center that you want to change for many months or years, then realize that it is going to take a one day at a time day by day repetition to change it! Upon rising each day, say to yourself, "just today I am going to do this," and do it! Before you know it, two days, three days, will pass. Then two months, three months, then you will start to see that it is working from the repetition. Then it will be two years, then three years, and then one day you will realize that you no longer like the old negative way, and the new way feels much better, and is your new good addiction! You can do it -God gave you your own will power through your control/power center, and yes he gave us others to help. Check with your doctor before trying any of these exercises. This philosophy is not a substitute for any professional medical care.

Chapter 33

DRUGS VERSUS COLORS AND YOUR SEVEN CENTERS

Drugs have very strong affects on us spiritually, mentally and physically. They affect certain chemicals in our brains. Drugs can be used to relax or stimulate us in many different ways. They can affect our seven centers, spiritual, mental, vocal, physical, control, emotional and sexual. There is much research going on concerning the affects of physical, and mental healing abilities of color therapy towards many parts of the human body. If our Name Colorology theories can someday be proven accurate by medical research and testing, a person may be able to use their center colors to affect their seven centers in a way such as drugs to stimulate or relax these centers. I have used my center colors to stimulate and relax myself and it works very well for myself, for example, I use one of my emotional/relax center colors, green. Also to relieve me of stress, when ever I walk into my green room it is almost like someone has given me a drug to relax me and my stressful feelings start to decline almost immediately. Just look at how some prisons use the color pink to neutralize aggressive behavior in inmates, they became very passive within a very short period of time. Or look how white full spectrum light is used to help for those living in parts of Alaska that are deprived of full spectrum sunlight for 6 months. Remember do not use any of the color formulas in this book as a substitute for any medical treatments, always check with your physician.

Homeopathic doctors talk about a person's dynamic force that possibly controls our immune system and has the ability to help heal and protect us from disease when our dynamic force is weakened. Can this dynamic force be our spiritual center color vibration force or our mental, vocal, physical, control, emotional, sexual vibrations, or a balance between them all? Is it as normally believed that our spiritual, physical or emotional state of being can cause disease or sickness to arise? Only time and testing will tell!

"The great importance of color lies in the fact that it can influence all different aspects of man-physical, mental and spiritual, and so help to produce that harmony which itself implies perfect health".

"The human body is composed of cells. The basis of life is the atom. Within the atom are vibrating particles-negatively charged- electrons circling around positively charge protons. Beyond this, color therapy postulates a rhythmic order of vibrations of several degrees, the lowest and coarsest being the physical, then the emotional, and then the mental. Health is harmony disease is discord. Illness may arise in the physical, emotional, or mental sphere".

"Is it too visionary to imagine a time when diseases will be classified by their wavelength and the counteracting of them become a mathematical certainty?" - J. Dodson Hessey

"Or can we say that our well being is determined by how well we cultivate God's Rainbow of positive character color traits that are attuned to our seven centers?"
- Baron Paul Greycastle

Chapter 34

GENERAL RULES AND USES OF YOUR CENTERS AND COLORS

I have one basic piece of advice on the use of your colors and centers and their traits. That is, as God has told us, "Use everything in moderation". Do not abuse your powers for selfish gains or excessive goals. One needs to cultivate all their centers and balance all these centers. If one center is to dominate, and other centers are not cultivated enough, it creates problems to our harmony and in being a balanced human being! Our centers are like gears in a clock; they are interdependent. If one center is off, it tends to throw off the whole clock. If you need to relax, then put the emphasis on your relaxing emotional center colors. If one needs to make practical and intelligent decisions then work on your intellectual center. Good luck, God bless, and always check with your doctor before using any of your centers or colors.

Chapter 35

THE BENEFITS OF NAME COLOROLOGY FOR EDUCATIONAL INSTITUTIONS

The main purpose of schools besides teaching students the basics of reading, writing, and arithmetic, is also to find out where their interests and talents are. Name Colorology has a great advantage in doing this because of its precise knowledge of each person's character traits and natural abilities. We have shown in this book how all the different color types dominate different fields, and believe our system is excellent for bringing out the best in students at any age. How many times have we heard the expression, "I should have cultivated my talents when I had a chance," or "It's a shame to let a good mind go to waste"? How can a teacher help a student cultivate their natural talents and genius if they do not know them, and especially when they have over a hundred students to cultivate at a time? Name Colorology can give them a great start and save them a great deal of time in doing so. Name Colorology also makes students aware that they have these seven centers and when they are operating off of them either negative or positive thus helping them to grow in a more mature and balanced manner. How many person's have we seen and known that had great talents in some area's of their personality but were terrible in other areas? Don't waste a child's talents, you can help them to tap into them very early in life.

Chapter 36

NAMING YOUR CHILDREN

Naming your children is a "very important" decision and has a tremendous affect on their personality. I would estimate our names affect 70% of our personality. Would you like your child to have a much greater chance of becoming a doctor, lawyer, writer, musician or any other profession? You can help to pre-determine any career and personality type! You can even give them a name that will make them more harmonious with you and their brothers or sisters by making sure the third sounding letters in their names are the same color type, for example: Da(n)ny and Do(n)nie or Sa(l)ly and Su(s)an. The (l) and the (s) are both yellow letters. In the case of Danny and Donnie both are blue harmony persons, Sally and Susan are both yellow harmony names. Once you know what their names are going to be you can also know what negative traits to steer them away from, for example take the name "Tommy." This person is a green spiritual, harmony and heart center person. You would have to guide this young man away from becoming the macho ego gangster personality type and routinely remind him of his positive traits of being peaceful, balanced, fair, lawful and agreeable. You could also help him to cultivate his natural genius career traits such as becoming a lawyer, architect, environmentalist, model, etc. Let me give another example: Willa Wade, this young lady is a double purple spiritual person because her first and last names start with (W) and she is also a purple mental person from the second letter (i) in her first name. I would highly advise exposing this young lady to the field of writing or the cultural arts. She could also do very well in any other field that is in tune with the purple spectrum traits, maturity, tastefulness, civilized, loyal, self sacrificing, dedicated, dignified, regal, idealistic, intuitive, cultured, and empowered. You could also steer her away from the negative traits of snobbishness, lack of taste, fanaticism, superiority, monopolization, treachery, pompousness, pettiness, domination, uncivilized, and undignified. The other great benefit of Name Colorology is you can also change a child's or adult's personality traits and talents by changing their name. Name Colorology gives a parent such a tremendous amount of knowledge into their children's personality it would be an absolute shame to waste it. Once again, we highly recommend that you have us here at the NameColorology Group do an initial reading of any name you want to be analyzed. Because of our 25 years of research and experience in this philosophy, we have seen many new users to the system make crucial mistakes that make all the difference between a correct and incorrect reading.

No better heritage can a father bequeath to his children than a good name; nor is there in a family any richer heir-loom than the memory of a noble ancestor. - J.Hamilton.

A name truly good is the aroma from virtuous character; it is a spontaneous emanation from genuine excellence. - Such a name is not only remembered on earth but in heaven. - J.Hamilton.

Good name, in man or women, is the immediate jewel of their souls. - Who steals my purse steals trash; but he that filches my good name, robs me of that which not enriches him, and makes me poor indeed. - Shakespeare.

Great names debase, instead of raising those who not no how to use them. - Rochefoucauld.

Chapter 37

PRICE LIST FOR NAME COLOROLOGY CONSULTING
SERVICES AND PRODUCTS

Name Colorology Book--- $ 25.00 U.S. - plus 3.95 shipping and handling
$39.95 Canada - plus 5.95 shipping and handling

Email and Telephone Consultaions:
www.namecolorology.com or 1-877-505-9100

3 Individual Questions---$ 10.00

5 Individual Questions---$ 16.00

7 Individual Questions---$ 25.00

Analysis for Your Wardrobe-Home-Decor-Romance Center/Colors---$43.00

Full Chart Analysis for Wardrobe-Home-Decor-Romance-Career ---$70.00

Example Questions:

• What color should I wear to stimulate my husband emotionally/romantically?

• What colors should I use in my home to have a relaxing affect on me?

• What colors should I wear to a job interview?

• What is a good name for my new baby if I want her or him to be a dancer, doctor, lawyer, etc.?

• I want to look younger, what center and colors should I cultivate and wear?

• My daughter is going to a prom, what color should she wear?

• What color should I wear to look glamorous and sexy or to stimulate my husband sexually?

• What color should I wear to stimulate my husband sexually?

• What center and color do I cultivate to break a bad habit?

• What are my son's genius traits for a career?

• What color should I wear to command more money in financial interviews etc.?

• Does this man's name harmonize with mine?

• How do I become more harmonious?

• What color do I wear to look more feminine and romantic?

Custom Wardrobe Designing---Call our 1-877-505-9100 Number to Inquire for Prices.

All Other Products And Services Are In Their Planning And Production Stages.

All Above Prices Are Subject To Changes

Chapter 38

NAME COLOROLOGY AND OUR ZERO TOLERANCE TOWARDS THE USE OF FUR, LEATHER AND OTHER ANIMAL PRODUCTS FOR BEAUTY, FASHION, AND HOME-DECOR!

We here at the Name Colorology Group are totally against the use of animal furs, leather, or any other animal products, that cause unnecessary pain and cruelty to animals . It is written that God gave us dominion over animals and we are convinced he did not mean cruel dominion, but "kind" dominion! Also, as stated at the beginning of this book, Mr. Greycastle says that all we have to do is look at God's example to save the different species of animals when he had Noah round them all up to save them from the flood. Just look at all the wonderful things they do for us, they give us friendship and company, they help the blind and handicap, they help rescue victims that are trapped along with warning us of intruders, and many times have saved people when their homes were on fire. There are some that refer to them as just wild animals. Well we have seen more wild animals trained in a very short and easier time to be peaceful and domesticated than a lot of wild mean people.

 The Name Colorology Group will be active in the fight to stop all cruelty to animals. We will be donating a percentage of all sales to this cause. We hope that you will support us in any way you can. We will keep you updated on our animal rights activities through our web site.

"A human being is a part of the whole called by us "universe," a part limited in time and space. He experiences himself, his thoughts and feelings as something separated from the rest, a kind of optical delusion of his consciousness. This delusion is a kind of prison for us, restricting us to free ourselves from this prison by widening our circle of, "compassion to embrace living creatures," and the whole of nature in it's beauty. Nobody is able to achieve this completely, but the striving for such achievement is in itself a part of the liberation and a foundation for inner security"- Albert Einstein

Do It Yourself Life-Long Color Chart

WARDROBE IMAGES						
CENTER	COLOR	COLOR	COLOR	IMAGE	IMAGE	IMAGE	IMAGE
SPIRITUAL							
MENTAL							
VOCAL							
PHYSICAL							
CONTROL							
EMOTIONAL							
SEXUAL							

HOME DECOR – MOOD ENVIRONMENTS						
CENTER	COLOR	COLOR	COLOR	ROOM	ROOM	ROOM	ROOM
SPIRITUAL							
MENTAL							
VOCAL							
PHYSICAL							
CONTROL							
EMOTIONAL							
SEXUAL							

CAREER ALTERNATIVES						
CENTER	COLOR	COLOR	COLOR	CAREER	CAREER	CAREER	CAREER
SPIRITUAL							
MENTAL							
VOCAL							
PHYSICAL							
CONTROL							
EMOTIONAL							
SEXUAL							

Do It Yourself Life-Long Color Chart

SAMPLE NAME: SANDY LARKON

WARDROBE IMAGES							
CENTER	COLOR	COLOR	COLOR	IMAGE	IMAGE	IMAGE	IMAGE
SPIRITUAL	yellow	yellow		youthful	creative	cheerful	
MENTAL	flesh	flesh		practical	logical		
VOCAL	blue	orange		fluent			
PHYSICAL	orange	orange		dramatic	assertive	physical	
CONTROL	blue	orange		corporate	refined	regal	formal
EMOTIONAL	red	violet	green	romantic	relaxed	feminine	
SEXUAL	orange	blue		sexy	earthy		

HOME DECOR – MOOD ENVIRONMENTS							
CENTER	COLOR	COLOR	COLOR	ROOM	ROOM	ROOM	ROOM
SPIRITUAL	yellow	yellow		kitchen	Rec.R.		
MENTAL	flesh	flesh		office	study	music	
VOCAL	blue	orange		music			
PHYSICAL	orange	orange		art studio	exercise		
CONTROL	blue	orange		dining	office		
EMOTIONAL	red	violet	green	bedroom	living	Patio	
SEXUAL	orange	blue		bedroom			

CAREER ALTERNATIVES							
CENTER	COLOR	COLOR	COLOR	CAREER	CAREER	CAREER	CAREER
SPIRITUAL	yellow	yellow		scientist	teacher		
MENTAL	flesh	flesh		finance	composer	manager	
VOCAL	blue	orange		opera			
PHYSICAL	orange	orange		potter	artist		
CONTROL	blue	orange		banker			
EMOTIONAL	red	violet	green	poet	ecologist		
SEXUAL	orange	blue		belly dancer			

166

ORDERING ANOTHER COPY OF NAME COLOROLOGY BOOK.

This book makes an excellent gift for relatives or friends. (approx. 25% of all sales of these books are given as gifts!) To order another copy or more: send $ 25.00 U.S. for each book of which a percentage will go to certain charitable organizations. (Add $ 3.95 for shipping and handling) $39.95 Canada - add $5.95 for shipping and handling) to:

Name Colorology Group
P. O. Box 21
Crockett, Ca. 94525

Name_____

Address_____

Telephone_____

Email address _____

You can also order our book at www.namecolorology.com
or call our toll free number 1-877-505-9100

To all of you who have enjoyed this book and would like to become involved with our company just come to our web site and read our, "Affiliates" page or just give us a call at the above toll free number---Thanks and God Bless!

To order another copy or more: send $ 25.00 U.S. for each book of which a percentage will go to certain charitable organizations. (Add $ 3.95 for shipping and handling) $39.95 Canada - add $5.95 for shipping and handling) to:

Name Colorology Group
P. O. Box 21
Crockett, Ca. 94525

Name_____

Address_____

Telephone_____

Email address _____